KU-203-142

THE COMPLETE GUIDE TO
LIFTING HEAVY WEIGHTS

Dr Geoffrey K. Platt

ANDOVER COLLEGE
STUDY CENTRE
613.713

ANDOVER COLLEGE

BLOOMSBURY

This book has been awarded 4 CPD points by the Register of Exercise Professionals. REPs requires that all instructors regularly update their skills and knowledge, which is evidenced by the recording of 12 CPD points per year. If you already hold an industry qualification you can answer the questions at the end of each chapter as part of your professional development. For further information please visit the REPs website at www.exerciseregister.org.

Whilst every effort has been made to ensure that the content of this book is as technically accurate and as sound as possible, neither the author nor the publishers can accept responsibility for any injury or loss sustained as a result of the use of this material.

Published in 2011 by
A&C Black Publishers Ltd
An imprint of Bloomsbury Publishing Plc
36 Soho Square, London W1D 3QY
www.acblack.com
www.bloomsbury.com

Copyright © Geoffrey K. Platt 2011

ISBN 978 1 4081 3325 5

All rights reserved. No part of this publication may be reproduced in any form or by any means – graphic, electronic or mechanical, including photocopying, recording, taping or information storage and retrieval systems – without the prior permission in writing of the publishers.

Geoffrey K. Platt asserted his right under the Copyright, Design and Patents Act, 1988, to be identified as the author of this work.

A CIP catalogue record for this book is available from the British Library.

Commissioned by Charlotte Croft
Designed by James Watson
Cover photograph © Getty Images
Photographs on pages 8, 13, 28, 29, 31, 33, 39, 46, 48 and 56 © Shutterstock
Photograph on page 2 © Getty Images
All other photographs © Darren Holloway
Illustrations on pages 10, 19, 20 and 53 by Greg Stevenson Illustrations
All other illustrations by David Gardner

This book is produced using paper that is made from wood grown in managed, sustainable forests. It is natural, renewable and recyclable. The logging and manufacturing processes conform to the environmental regulations of the country of origin.

Typeset in 10.75pt on 14pt Adobe Caslon by Saxon Graphics Ltd, Derby

Printed and bound in India by Replika Press Pvt Ltd

ANDOVER COLLEGE

066145

WITHDRAWN

THE COMPLETE GUIDE TO
LIFTING HEAVY WEIGHTS

CONTENTS

ACKNOWLEDGEMENTS

During a long and privileged career that has included weightlifting, powerlifting, strength and conditioning, fitness training, strength events, highland gatherings and heavy athletics, I have been honoured to have been coached, instructed, tutored and advised by some great men. I refer to men like Oscar State, Wally Holland, Hymie Binder, John Lear, Al Murray, Tamas Ajan, Gottfried Schodl, Vic Mercer, David Webster, Tom McNab and Wilf Paish. These men taught me a great deal about life, strength and the use of force, and for that I am eternally grateful.

I have enjoyed the privilege to work with some of the greatest athletes in the world in these sports, and again, I have learned from every one of them. Unfortunately there are too many to name. Each has been a strong character as well as an exceptionally strong athlete and they taught me what men have known for many centuries:

> That intelligence and skill can only function at the peak of their capacity when the body is healthy and strong; that hardy spirits and tough minds usually inhabit sound bodies.
>
> John F. Kennedy, 1960

I would like to express my appreciation to those who have helped me to improve my academic knowledge of these subjects, Mike Stone, Dave Collins and most of all to John Sproule, who together helped me to achieve my doctorate at the University of Edinburgh. Special thanks also goes to George Byng and Charles Revolta, who both assisted me by reviewing this book.

Finally, may I express my appreciation to my family, to my wife Annette and my daughters, Jenni, Laura and Ella, who have supported me throughout my career.

Geoff Platt, 2011

W.S.N. (Wales, Scotland and Northern Ireland)   Wales Weightlifting   Weightlifting Scotland   Northern Ireland Weight Lifters Association

These are the National Governing Bodies for the sport of Weightlifting in these countries, as recognised by the International Weightlifting Federation.

INTRODUCTION

The lifting of weights is an extremely popular way to keep fit for many people. Weights are relatively inexpensive and allow large numbers of people to train together in a small area in relative comfort.

Going to the gym is seen by many people as a very sociable activity where they can meet their friends, build up a sweat, relieve the stresses of the week and get fit. Gyms are warm, bright, welcoming places which are open at times that suit busy people, whether it be early morning, late evening, at weekends, or during the working day for shift workers. They can work out with friends or focus on their personal training, and they can seek advice about their programme, their diet or their lifestyle from experts.

But lifting weights means different things to different people. Some people lift weights to get strong; some to get bulkier; some to get smaller; some to get fitter; some to get fatter; some people may want to recover after an injury; some may want to cope with a disability. A gym is a place where you can build the body that you want. For this reason, it can be a very personal place.

HISTORY

The history of lifting weights goes back several thousand years, with evidence that early man competed with his neighbours to test his strength by lifting stones. It was Hippocrates, the 'Father of Modern Medicine', who introduced science to the sport when he wrote 'that which is used develops, and that which is not used wastes away'. The ancient Greeks, with their love of sport and their belief in the importance of the human body, developed the subject further and it was Milo of Croton who first illustrated the principles of progressive resistance training, which are set out in chapter 1.

Gaining strength remained the objective of all lifting of weights until the second half of the 19th century. It was at about this time that there was an increase in interest in health and exercise. The 'physical culture movement' used weights to get fit, to strengthen their skeletons and to develop their muscles. Physical culturalists tested their strength, but lifting heavy weight was not their *raison d'être*.

Russian heavyweight weightlifter Yuri Vlasov in action during the 1962 World Championships, which he won to achieve the official title of strongest man in the world

expanded until, in 1988, the East German Olympic Committee required that all athletes seeking selection for the Olympic Games, irrespective of their sport, undertake a programme of Olympic Weightlifting designed to improve the explosive extension of the hip, knee and ankle. These actions are all components of the running, jumping, throwing and kicking that are a part of almost every sport. The only sport that is an exception is sailing.

Also in the 1960s, governments around the world started to recognise the positive value of sport and exercise to the health of a nation, as well as to its financial well-being. Accordingly, many started to introduce 'sport for all' policies that saw the introduction of publicly funded community sports centres that usually included one of the newly designed multigyms. Soon it became acceptable for all sections of the community to participate in lifting weights in order to improve their health and fitness. In practice, this meant women and young people starting to use the new gyms and it focused attention on the whole range of components of fitness, from strength to endurance, muscular endurance, flexibility, speed, fitness and body composition.

The lifting of weights underwent fundamental changes in the late 1950s and early 1960s. This started when Oscar State, the General Secretary of the International Weightlifting Federation (IWF), got together with the British Athletics Coach, Geoff Dyson, to write a book entitled *Weightlifting for Athletics*. It advocated the use of lifting weights to improve performance in athletics and over the following years the lifting of weights to improve sporting performance

LIFTING WEIGHTS TODAY

There are five competitive sports and contests that revolve around lifting weights. They are:

1. WEIGHTLIFTING

Otherwise known as Olympic Weightlifting, this is contested at all levels, from the Olympic Games, World Championships and Commonwealth Games to continental, national, regional and local championships.

Weightlifting consists of the two overhead lifts: the *snatch* and the *clean and jerk*. An athlete is awarded three attempts at each exercise on a rising bar (one on which the weight is only permitted to remain the same or to increase) and the best successful attempt at each exercise is added together to give a total that determines the winner.

Olympic weightlifting records*

- The world record for the snatch is 213kg or 470lbs
- The world record for the clean and jerk is 263kg or 580lbs

2. POWERLIFTING

Powerlifting is contested at World Championships and at continental, national, regional and local championships.

Powerlifting consists of the three strength lifts: the *squat*, the *bench press* and the *dead lift*. An athlete is awarded three attempts at each exercise and the athletes all take their first attempts, second attempts and third attempts. The best successful attempt at each exercise is added together to give a total that determines the winner.

Powerlifting records*

- The world record for the squat is 457.5kg or 1007lbs
- The world record for the bench press is 352.5kg or 777lbs
- The world record for the dead lift is 408kg or 898lbs

*Note: On 1/1/11, bodyweight classes changed; these are the records for the unlimited bodyweight category.

3. BODYBUILDING

Bodybuilding is about creating the perfectly shaped body, with each part of the body developed and in proportion to the rest of the body. Weights are not lifted in competition, which involves posing to show your shape to best effect, but are used to build the body.

Bodybuilding is effectively run by companies who organise tournaments where they feel that there is a need.

There are also other activities that require a considerable amount of strength training in order for people to compete in them:

4. 'STRONGEST MAN' CONTESTS

These are contests usually run for television where all the competitors usually hold titles from previous participation in powerlifting competitions. Events usually include squats, dead lifts, overhead lifts, barrel or stone lifts and truck or aeroplane pulls.

5. HIGHLAND GATHERINGS

These are traditional events held all over Scotland and other places in the world with a Scottish community. Events include caber, Scottish hammer, 28lb (13kg) weight for distance, 56lb (26kg) weight for height and shot putt. Many weightlifters, powerlifters and athletic throwers participate.

GYM INSTRUCTION

The building of new community sports centres and the rapid expansion of the numbers of people using the gyms coincided with a Government initiative to move away from academic qualifications, based on a knowledge of theory, towards vocational qualifications which focused on practical skills. The British Amateur Weight Lifters Association (BAWLA) was approached by the Sports Council on behalf of the Department for Education and asked to adapt their Teachers Award course for weightlifting coaches into a new course for fitness instructors.

Later SPRITO (the Sport and Recreation Industry Training Organisation), now called Skills Active, was set up to bring together employers in the fitness industry to agree professional standards for those working in the industry. It standardised the awards so that there was a Level 2 Fitness Instructor Award (roughly equivalent to a GCSE) and a Level 3 Personal Trainer Award (roughly equivalent an A-level). It also changed the syllabuses for the courses by increasing the required knowledge of diet, nutrition, weight control, endurance, fitness etc, and generally reduced the content on specifically lifting heavy weights, in order to cater for the new market which consisted of increasing numbers of women and young people.

Many gym instructors have recently expressed the feeling that there has been a recent resurgence in the popularity of lifting weights in order to improve, and test, strength. Recently, there have been a number of incidents in which athletes have been injured while using heavy weights, which indicates that the quality of coaching and support available to those wishing to use heavy weights has fallen and that more work is needed to raise standards.

A review of the fitness industry has revealed a need to expand the training courses available to fitness instructors and personal trainers who want to assist those people who want to lift heavy weights. SkillsActive has accredited these courses as Continuing Professional Development (CPD) for those working in the industry and for those who want to work with

CYQ Level 2 Certificate in Fitness Instructing (gym-based exercise)

Unit description

Anatomy and physiology for exercise

Health, safety and welfare in a fitness environment

Principles of exercise, fitness and health

Know how to support clients who take part in exercise and physical activity

Planning gym-based exercise

Instructing gym-based exercise

CYQ Level 3 Certificate in Personal Training

In addition to units 2–4 above, learners need to complete:

Unit description

Anatomy and physiology for exercise and health

Applying the principles of nutrition as part of a personal training programme

Programming personal training with clients

Delivering personal training sessions

the athletes looking to improve their strength for whatever reason.

The syllabus for the new courses has been written by the author of this book, which itself has been written to support the courses and to provide a reference for those taking them. The areas covered in the new courses will include:

Techniques of the exercises

The heavier that the weight gets, the better that the technique needs to be.

Training methods and recovery methods

Advanced training methods and advanced recovery methods are required to lift the heaviest weights.

Safety

While all weights need to be treated with respect and handled with care, this is especially so when lifting the heaviest weights, where death and serious injury await those who fail to deal with them properly.

Drugs

It is no longer acceptable for professional coaches and instructors to brush aside questions relating to drugs in sport. This is an important issue that can result in imprisonment, suspension and humiliation in the press. Care must be exercised when taking any medication, as the World Anti-Doping Agency (WADA) list contains some medications available in petrol stations and newsagents, as well as those available only on prescription.

Welcome to the *Complete Guide to Lifting Heavy Weights*!

THE PRINCIPLES
// OF TRAINING

1

INTRODUCTION

In order to lift heavy weights, it is necessary to undertake long periods of regular, i.e. daily, hard training, and to lift progressively heavier weights while improving or at least maintaining all the other aspects of fitness. This will require a disciplined lifestyle in which attention is paid to early bedtimes, a balanced and healthy diet and moderate living. It will also require consideration to be given to doing everything possible in order to speed up recovery from training.

The strongest lifters in the world have traditionally come from Russia, Bulgaria and Eastern Europe and these athletes typically undertake five training sessions each day for six days each week, with one rest day to allow them to recover from their training. This level of training needs to be built up slowly or it will very quickly cause an athlete to collapse with exhaustion rather than significantly improve their strength.

This book is going to look at the principles of sports science that apply to training and recommend ways in which they can be implemented in a training programme designed to maximise strength gains. It must, however, be borne in mind that every person is an individual with their own strengths and weaknesses; the application of these principles will be very much a bespoke process for the athlete and his or her coach.

THE ATHLETE TODAY

Every training programme should revolve around the athlete. Each person is different, with different strengths and weaknesses, and these must be taken into consideration when designing his or her ideal training programme. It is good practice to begin by measuring the athlete in every way that comes to mind: physically, physiologically and even psychologically. The table on the opposite page shows one way in which this can be done, but you can add to this in any way that you think is appropriate. Be honest and do not gloss over any weaknesses. Use them to help build the athlete instead.

At this point, the athlete will probably have completed some training already and you should review their strengths and weaknesses, and their likes and dislikes, in the work that they have done so far.

Know your athlete

Topic	Notes
Name	
Age	
Actual age	
Developmental age	
Training age	
Gender	
Occupation	
Height	
Weight	
Skill	
Experience	
Fitness	
Injuries	
Illnesses	
Other sporting activities	
Contact details	
Mother	
Father	
Grandparents	
Performance	

THE FUTURE CHAMPION

An athlete should give some consideration to what they will have to look like and what they will have to be able to do if they are to be a champion. Many 16–18-year-old young men decide that they want to become sports champions. They are often tall and skinny when they make this decision, and if they are 1.83m/6'0" tall and weigh 75kg/11st 8lb, experience tells us that they will have to put on a considerable amount of weight, preferably muscle, before they start to win medals and titles.

Aspiring athletes should look at those who are achieving what they themselves want to achieve in the future. What height and weight are their role models? Athletes should make notes of what they see. In all likelihood, they will have to be roughly the same size and shape in order to achieve the same or better results in the future.

It may be at this time that an athlete realises that they are unlikely to achieve their ambitions and that they may need to review, and possibly change, them. It is better for an athlete to do that now, rather than realise after 10 years of hard work that they were never going to achieve their initial goals and that they have wasted a great deal of time and effort in attempting to achieve the impossible.

Many very tall athletes have considered becoming champion weightlifters before realising that few Olympic champions in weightlifting are much over 1.83m/6'0 tall, even in the heavy and super-heavyweight classes. If you are a little over this norm then you can simply be a tall weightlifter who trains hard, but if you are well over this norm, you must decide either to be the best that you can be as a weightlifter, or you must seek an alternative: many young men in this position have decided to take up shot putting, discus throwing or hammer throwing etc, where taller men have been more successful.

THE TRAINING ROUTE

The athlete, having fixed two points in their life (where they are now and where they want to be in the future), can start to give some thought to the route that they will need to take in order to achieve their goals. This does not mean that the route is set in stone and cannot be changed, but it does give the programme a serious sense of direction until it is varied. A good example of this process is a story that has often been repeated about Mark Foster, the Olympic swimmer. It is said that he returned home after a Commonwealth Games disappointed at his performance and worried that he needed to improve his time by one second if he was to win the Olympic Games in a little more than a year. He decided that he was likely to compete in 25 races during that year leading up to the Olympics and that he needed to improve his time by 0.04 seconds (1.00 second ÷ 25 races) in each race in order to achieve his goal.

The calculations that most athletes make will be considerably more difficult than the one set out above, for a number of very good reasons. The most difficult factor is that a substantial proportion of young men making a decision to commit to becoming champions are less than 18–21 years of age and therefore may not have completely finished their final growth spurt, so they may grow taller. The second factor is that most tasks get harder as we continue them, so that the initial progress is rapid, but will diminish as we continue, so we should not rely on relentless progress. The third factor is that, for a variety of reasons, certain elements in our progress need to be undertaken at certain stages of our development or training and, if training time is limited, then other elements may have to be deferred to fit them in.

A good example of an element being focused upon at a particular stage of development or training is flexibility. Up to approximately 16 years of age, most young men will accept the advice of their coach and undertake the training that they are given to do. After this time, they will often reject advice and refuse to complete the training that they are given. Coaches who are aware of this problem will set up a training programme to prioritise flexibility training at an early stage of the athlete's development, so that it is not such a problem if the athlete cuts back on it later. If the coach fails to recognise this problem and the athlete then refuses to complete the flexibility training, then the athlete's prospects will be severely diminished. Another area where athletes may be reluctant to work is repetitive technique training, which they often find boring.

THE COMPONENTS OF FITNESS

When identifying the training route, the athlete and coach need to consider each of the components of fitness.

STRENGTH

Definition: The ability to lift a maximum weight or overcome a maximum resistance for a single repetition.
Examples: The best examples are powerlifters and weightlifters.

ENDURANCE

Definition: The ability to keep on exercising for a prolonged period of time.
Examples: Marathon runners and triathletes.

MUSCULAR ENDURANCE

Definition: The ability to keep on working one or more muscles for a prolonged period of time.
Examples: Tug of war and arm wrestling.

FITNESS

Definition: The ability to recover after exertion.
Examples: Football players and boxers who are able to rest between runs or rounds.

SPEED

Definition: The ability to move at the highest speed.
Examples: Sprinters (who move the body along the track) and throwers (who move their arms).

FLEXIBILITY

Definition: The ability to move a joint through the widest range of movement.
Examples: Gymnasts and hurdlers.

BODY COMPOSITION

Definition: The amount of fat in the body, usually expressed as a percentage.
Example: Bodybuilders.

Not only does each sport require a different blend and balance of each of these components, but each athlete will also require an individual blend and balance, depending on their physiology, physique and technique. These components of fitness relate to each other as set out in figure 1.1 (overleaf).

At this point we should have decided on the changes to the physique and physiology that the athlete needs to make in order to become a champion and we can now start to consider the best ways to go about making these changes.

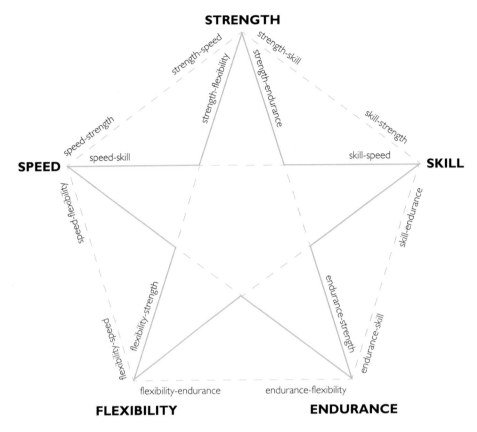

Figure 1.1 Relationship between the components of fitness

THE PRINCIPLES OF TRAINING

All training must be:

PROGRESSIVE

Definition: Continuously getting harder as the athlete adapts to it.

Explanation: In ancient Greece there was a man called Milo of Croton. His father was a farmer and owned a cow. The cow had a calf and Milo made a point of lifting the calf onto his back in order to get stronger. Over the next two years the calf grew into a full grown cow and Milo grew into a weightlifter. There was no way that Milo would ever have lifted a cow unless he had started with the calf and trained up.

SPECIFIC

Definition: All training must be focused on the goals to be achieved.

Explanation: There is very little point in an ambitious young weightlifter running a marathon in training. His endurance will improve, but it will not reflect in his ability to get stronger and lift more.

VARIED

Definition: Training requires a certain breadth.

Example: While training needs to be specific to the task, to select just one exercise and work on it several times each day to the exclusion of everything else will soon become very boring and result in a drop in motivation. It will also result in a very narrow type of strength.

PLANNED

Definition: Each session needs to build on the previous one and prepare for the next one.
Explanation: Anecdotal evidence suggests that the former East German coaches celebrated an athlete reaching puberty by presenting them with a printed diary of the proposed training sessions for the next 12 years. These would only vary in cases of injury.

It should be remembered however that, unfortunately, all training is:

REVERSIBLE

Definition: All training gains are lost in approximately a third of the time that it took to make them.
Explanation: Training needs to be relentless. It is not possible to train hard, and take breaks for holidays or parties. The benefits of three weeks hard work will be lost if the athlete then misses training to go on holiday, or as a result of an injury. He or she has simply wasted the coach's time and his or her own time.

It is now necessary to set a timescale for these targets to be achieved. Coaches and athletes need to consider their ambitions and when these can reasonably be achieved. It may be that the athlete has set his or her heart on winning an Olympic gold medal. Olympic Games only take place every four years and it will be necessary to identify which Games the athlete can reasonably expect to target, so that training can be arranged accordingly.

LONG-TERM GOALS

As a result of the planning undertaken so far, a number of targets should have been set. A very simple example may look something like the table on page 12.

Although a very simple example, this set of goals covers each of the components of fitness set out above. It is accepted that an endurance runner would not consider a 400m run as an endurance activity, but it is in the context of a weightlifter. All young people need to develop their hearts and lungs and achieve reasonable levels of fitness, and it is interesting that at a recent UK Athletics seminar the world champions for each of the throwing events (the shot, discus, hammer and javelin) all announced that they regularly ran 10,000m cross-country runs every month, despite their bodyweight being over 125kg.

The scores for flexibility and fitness reflect a personalised programme for each individual athlete in which his or her range of motion is measured in a range of specific exercises.

Some targets do not require the athlete to improve to achieve them, but may require considerable effort in order to maintain them. Many young men can eat anything and still maintain a body composition of 10% bodyfat at 16 years of age. If those young men then double their bodyweight by training, they will clearly struggle to keep their bodyfat at 10%. The same young men may find it easy to run a lap of a track in 60 seconds as a 16-year-old at 70kg, but considerably harder as an adult at 140kg. These are extreme examples set out to make a specific point.

Setting long-term goals			
Goal	Category	At 16 years	At 26 years
Height	Development	1.70m	1.80m
Weight	Development	70kg	120kg
Best clean	Strength	60kg	180kg
Best jerk	Strength	65kg	190kg
Best snatch	Strength	40kg	140kg
Best squat	Strength	70kg	220kg
Dead lift hold	Muscular endurance in grip	20 sec	40 sec
Best 40m run	Speed	4 sec	3.5 sec
Best 400m run	Endurance	60 sec	60 sec
Body composition	Body composition	10%	10%
Flexibility score	Flexibility	67	80
Fitness score	Fitness	70	80

SHORT-TERM GOALS

Specific annual targets should be set for each of the interim years, so that progress may be monitored regularly and effort and focus adjusted accordingly. At this stage, consideration should be given as to whether the improvements required by the programme are seriously achievable or whether they need to be reset. If this is not done then disappointment will inevitably be the result in the future.

These targets should be agreed publicly so that both sides have ownership of them. Failure to achieve these goals may result in the breakdown of the relationship between athlete and coach, but both parties need to be aware of the current situation at all stages of the relationship.

LIFESTYLE

In designing a programme for an athlete, a great deal of factors need to be taken into consideration by the coach or trainer. Clearly all the targets need to be met, but there also needs to be: balance between improving fitness and improving technique; a removal of overlap; opportunities to recover from the training; and opportunities to compete during training.

None of this is worth undertaking until the athlete accepts that first and foremost his or her lifestyle must change. Until the 1980s, there was an acceptance among young athletes that they had to tolerate a Spartan existence and most of them were proud of this. Recent press coverage of professional sportsmen and women partying late into the night has confused many young athletes, who now fail to recognise the value of a healthy lifestyle.

Recently I drove three athletes to a competition. These were young men hoping to achieve selection for the Junior World Championships later in the year. On the way home after the competition one started making calls on his mobile phone to hire DVDs for when he returned. Another placed orders for jerk chicken and pizza and bottles of carbonated drinks. The third placed orders for recreational drugs. They did all this, without thought, in front of a man who would play a key role in their future selections.

I questioned these athletes and they happily admitted that they seldom got to bed before 3a.m. due to friends calling, watching DVDs and playing computer games. They often ate junk food, drank carbonated drinks and took recreational drugs. They were very surprised when told to change their lifestyle or give up training as they were wasting their time. These young men, unsurprisingly, failed to make the progress that they needed to and were not selected for the championships at the end of the season. They had trained for four hours a day but their hard work had been sabotaged by their lifestyle.

Stories in the press are invariably about athletes who are famous and who have already achieved many of their goals. As athletes in this position, they can afford to miss the odd session and celebrate their success without it affecting their performance, which is based on several years of hard work.

LIFESTYLE ISSUES

These can include:

Sensible bedtimes

There is an old wives' tale which says that an hour asleep in bed before midnight is worth two hours after midnight, but there is a great deal of truth in it. Athletes do need at least eight hours sleep each night, usually more with all the training that they are doing. It is essential to remove all the technology in their bedrooms that prevent sleep, such as mobile telephones, computers and

televisions, or at the very least ensure that they are all switched off.

Daytime rest breaks

Many athletes take rest breaks in the middle of the day: for sleep, or just resting on the bed, or maybe some active rest, like watching videos or playing on the computer, which rests the body while the mind remains active. The need for these breaks obviously increases as the training load increases above one session per day.

Healthy meals

A hard-working athlete will need a healthy supply of food. It should contain a good balance of all types of nutrients, including proteins, fats, carbohydrates, vitamins, minerals, roughage and water. It is advised that most people drink 1.5 litres of water each day, but this should be roughly double for athletes, due to the sweat produced during training.

Keep the right balance of food to get all the nutrients you need

It should not be surprising that, when they train, athletes often find that their appetite increases. This is not a problem as it indicates that the food is needed to provide the energy required to train. A good way to provide essential energy is by eating carbohydrates such as pasta. This should not, however, be used as an excuse for gluttony and increases in bodyfat should be avoided. Try to include plenty of fresh fruit and salad and to reduce junk foods, as well as other fatty and sugary foods. As time goes by, an athlete should seek specialist advice from a nutritionist.

Controlled snacking

Many experienced athletes take a supply of food and water with them when they go training. The food is often something simple such as 50mg of dried fruit or a banana, which provides fuel after training in order to re-energise for the next session.

Mental relaxation

Some training requires little mental effort while causing total physical exhaustion. As a result, some athletes like to lie down and watch a DVD or play a computer game, so that the body is resting while the brain is working. This is a matter of personal choice.

Happy home life

Few things cause as much stress as living in an unhappy home, and few homes are happy 100% of the time. This is a particular problem before or during a major competition.

Good family relationships

A major component of a good home life is good family relationships. If these are problematic then the athlete should be told, sensitively, that they should be dealt with as soon as possible, or they will remain to sabotage performance in the future.

Good work life

Only a little way behind a happy home life is happiness at the other place where we spend the majority of our time, at work. Again, problems here need to be resolved or will remain to sabotage performance in the future.

Happy student life

The situation is no different for those still at school, college or university.

Strong financial situation

A wide range of grants and sponsorships are available to young athletes and these need to be investigated to reduce potential financial obstructions.

Avoidance of stress

Steps to avoid stress and remove potential causes of stress need to be taken at an early stage.

Avoidance of drinking alcohol

While an occasional and small drink is not a problem, anything more than that should be avoided. A single binge-drinking session is likely to ruin a good week's training.

Avoidance of drugs

Athletes should be aware of the consequences of drugs on their body and on their performance. They should also be very clear that athletes are subject to drug testing at any time, whether in or out of competition. Failure to comply with a test or recording a positive result will conclude in severe negative publicity and likely humiliation, and may end a promising career.

Avoidance of smoking

One cigarette leads to another. Tobacco can lead to cannabis. Smoking results in nothing positive and, as HM Government states on every packet of cigarettes, 'Smoking kills'.

Healthy living

This involves a moderate lifestyle and sexual moderation. Clearly, young ladies will need to be able to manage the health and lifestyle issues that affect them.

As the athlete develops and matures, the coach will have to remain cogniscent of all these matters and monitor issues that arise in order that they may be managed to the best effect.

PROGRAMME DESIGN

Clear evidence exists which asserts that more athletes currently over-train than under-train (*see* Silva III, J. M., in bibliography); coaches have to carefully identify the amount of time available for training after essential issues have been taken into consideration, like the availability of training venues and the training priorities, as well as future competitions and the priority that must be given for them.

A basic programme will identify the parts of the body that require most work. An advanced programme, prepared by a more knowledgeable coach, will look at which muscle groups require the most work and the sequence in which these muscles are most likely to be used, so that the programme may reflect these factors.

A simple programme should reflect the components of fitness and their priority to the athlete's future performance. An advanced programme should identify specific fitness targets that must be achieved by the athlete.

EXAMPLE OF A SIMPLE TRAINING PROGRAMME (POSSIBLY BY A LEVEL 2 COACH)

Athlete

A 16-year-old schoolboy shot putter. Has been a member of school football team, but with little other fitness background.

Arranging a training programme with a young athlete without first consulting his or her parents is likely to lead to serious problems in the future. By consulting with parents, discussing their plans and the athlete's plans, hopefully these problems can be avoided. A case occurred a few years ago in which the coach met the family and prepared detailed plans for the athlete's future that were agreed by all present. Things went well for three years until the athlete announced that he had been conscripted into the army of his home country and intended to comply. Two years were spent in the army and by the time the athlete returned, his plans for an athletic future were in ruins. Investigate all aspects of the athlete's future.

Time

It has been agreed between coach, athlete and parents that he will attend training three times each week, the minimum number of sessions for consistent progress. Each session will last between one and two hours and be followed by a rest day. The conventional Monday, Wednesday and Friday route would appear appropriate if it suits school homework, family commitments, facility availability and the commitments of both the athlete and coach.

Place

For a young athlete technique is important, so one session each week will be on technique and two will focus on improving the components of fitness. All may be performed in the school gymnasium.

Goals

In view of the youth of the performer and the level of the coach, no long-term plans have yet been made and training is focused on a general improvement of fitness and technique.

The coach is aware that shot putting is 60% legs and back and 40% upper body, and will attempt to reflect this in his or her programme. The coach is also aware that shot putting is largely a strength activity, but that the athlete struggles to complete the 50 throws that he or she is asked to perform in the technique session and cannot yet complete the standard fitness programme, so will set endurance as the priority at this stage, but hopes to be able to change this to strength as endurance improves.

Recovery

With an athlete of this age and lack of training experience, and with a coach of this qualification level, the session should be relatively gentle, so that the athlete might feel a little sore and tired the next day, but should have no lasting effects on the second day after training, when another session is planned. If there are any lasting effects from the first session then the athlete should refrain from training and stick to gentle stretching, which allows him or her to meet friends and do something while recovering. If this happens, then the next session should take this experience into consideration and should, therefore, be even more gentle.

After a few weeks of completing this training regime, experiencing no ill-effects and always being totally recovered from a session before being expected to perform another, then consideration may be given to a gentle increase of the work being asked of the athlete.

In this way, the athlete should continue to make slow, steady progress for many years, until old age becomes an issue.

The process

- The sessions will be Monday, Wednesday and Friday from 7p.m. to 9p.m. at the school gymnasium.
- Each session will start with a 15-minute warm-up and a 15-minute warm-down.
- The purpose of the warm-up is to prepare for exertion and to reduce the risk of injury. A warm-up session has three objectives:
  1. to raise body temperature by $1°C$ and gently increase heart rate;
  2. to stretch the muscles to be used in the session;

3. to mentally prepare for what you are going to do.

- A warm-down session is designed to return the body to rest and to calm the athlete. A warm-down session has three objectives:
1. to lower body temperature and heart rate gradually;
2. to relax the muscles that have been used in the session;
3. to mentally relax and calm after the session.
- After the warm-up, it is usual to start with technique work while the athlete is fresh.
- After the technique work, it is usual to move on to fitness work. This athlete required 60% legs and lower back and 40% upper body and was going to start by focusing on the endurance that he lacked.
- Most young athletes like to finish with a training competition before they warm down.

This process gives us a programme that looks like this:

Monday, Wednesday and Friday 7p.m. to 9p.m. at the school gymnasium.

- Warm-up (jogging/stretching/focusing on session)
- Technique work
- Fitness work (fartlek session/join in at end of circuit training/stretching)
- Training competition on standing shot put. Best of six throws.
- Warm-down

EXAMPLE OF AN ADVANCED TRAINING PROGRAMME

Athlete

A 16-year-old schoolboy shot putter. Has been a member of school football team, but with little other fitness background.

Time

It has been agreed between coach, athlete and parents that he will attend training three times each week, the minimum number of sessions for consistent progress. Each session will last between one and two hours and be followed by a rest day. The conventional Monday, Wednesday and Friday route would appear appropriate if it suits school homework, family commitments, facility availability and the commitments of athlete and coach.

Place

For a young athlete technique is important, so one session each week will be on technique and two will focus on improving the components of fitness. All may be performed in the school gymnasium.

Goals

A full fitness assessment has been performed by the coach and it is clear that the athlete does not yet have the fitness and endurance to undertake the amount of training that he or she needs. A target has been set by the coach, and agreed by the athlete, for the athlete to complete 1 lap of the circuit training by week 4, 2 laps by week 10 and 3 laps by week 16. This will then allow 16 weeks' work on technique before the 16-week competitive season, and the 4-week autumn break before next year's programme starts.

The coach has also completed a full strength assessment and identified that the athlete, like many 16-years-olds, has reasonable leg strength from running and playing football and other school sports, but almost no upper-body strength. The coach also recognises that the shot put requires good upper-body strength, particularly in the back of the upper arm and across the chest, in order to let all regions of the upper-body work together.

It will also be necessary to strengthen the muscles of the fingers, hands and wrists in order to avoid injury while throwing. In accordance with the plan, specific targets have been set to improve strength and achieve the goals that have been set in each particular area of weakness.

Recovery

While the athlete is young, the coach is experienced and should be able to judge the amount of work that the athlete can manage; although the training sessions might make the athlete feel a little sore and tired the next day, they should have no lasting effect on the second day after training, when another session is planned. If there are any lasting effects from the first session then the athlete should refrain from training and stick to gentle stretching, which allows him to meet his friends and do something while recovering. If this happens, then the next session should take this experience into consideration and should, therefore, be even more gentle.

After a few weeks of completing this training, experiencing no ill-effects and always being totally recovered from a session before being expected to perform another, then consideration may be given to a gentle increase of the work being asked of the athlete.

In this way, the athlete should continue to make good progress for many years, until old age becomes an issue.

The process

Will lead to a more intensive training session due to the knowledge and experience of the coach and will lead to better progress as a result.

Recovery

One of the main differences between coaches at advanced level concerns recovery after training. Many athletes believe that if one session is good for you, then two sessions are twice as good for you, and so on. This is why there is a tendency to over-train. In fact, if athletes do overtrain then their performance will deteriorate until they eventually collapse and take a rest, so that they recover that way.

When Ivan Abajiev, the coach to the Bulgarian weightlifting team that won the World Championships each year from 1970 to 1990, was asked what the difference was between the Bulgarian team and the British team, he surprised everyone by saying that the British team overtrained. As the British team generally trained either once or twice a day and the Bulgarian team trained five times a day, a few of the coaches present were surprised by his opinion, but he went on to explain that his team had excellent medical support and each member was regularly checked and tested.

Any athlete in the Bulgarian team who trained five times each and every day was expected to be in peak condition and, as such, should not be suffering from colds or flu. If they displayed any symptoms or complained of feeling unwell then they were sent by the coach to see the doctor.

Blood and urine tests were taken and they were stopped from undertaking any further training until the problem had been resolved.

An athlete injured while training was immediately sent out of the training hall. The athlete then went to take a shower at his or her personal shower. Although the Bulgarian team did not possess great wealth they had invested in personal showers for every lifter. Each shower had been personally adjusted for temperature and power, so that it was as hot and as hard as that athlete could manage. This meant that the shower had the effect of giving the athlete a massage and helping the warm-down process of relaxing muscles and assisting to clear lactic acid produced while training. The athlete then dried him- or herself off with a very rough towel, to complete the process.

The athlete then went to a rest room, where they could take a drink from a fridge that would help them to rehydrate and feed themselves, another stage of recovery after training. They could then relax and watch television until the other athletes finished training and took their showers, when the coach would come and discuss their injury. If the coach and athlete were satisfied that after the shower and short rest the injury was insignificant, the athlete resumed his original programme for the week. If there was any doubt about the injury, arrangements were made for the athlete to be seen by a doctor and to receive immediate treatment, and training would not be resumed until all parties were satisfied that all necessary treatment and rehabilitation had been completed. If the athlete received a second injury within two weeks, even if it was felt to be insignificant, the athlete was sent home from the training camp for two weeks as this was considered to be a warning of an impending crisis that might well lead to a more serious injury that could cause the athlete to miss training for a prolonged period.

A British athlete who tries to stop training without at least a broken leg is likely to face abuse from his training colleagues and eventually resume training without a break. This, of course, could then result in a serious injury and a prolonged disturbance of training.

Figure 1.2 shows the effect on performance of a single training session. Everybody is an individual, with their own level of fitness and their own ability to recover, which is why the graph has no scale assigned to it. After a single training session, athletes use words such as 'tired', 'exhausted', 'shattered', 'stiff', 'sore', 'knackered' and 'aching' to describe the way that they feel. Even after a good night's rest most athletes still feel the same way the next day. Only after a second night's rest do most report that they have recovered from training and feel that they are ready to undertake another session. There is then a short period when the athlete's performance improves as a result of the training session and they overcompensate to reach a new peak of performance on the graph. Later their performance tails off, but by then they have usually undertaken another training session, which tends to confuse the issue.

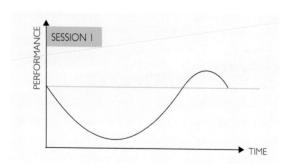

Figure 1.2 Effect on performance of a single training session

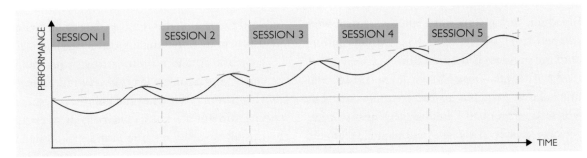

Figure 1.3 Effect on performance of training again at the optimum time

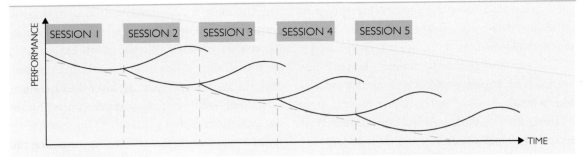

Figure 1.4 Effect on performance of training too soon

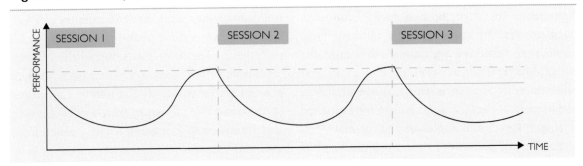

Figure 1.5 Effect on performance of training too late

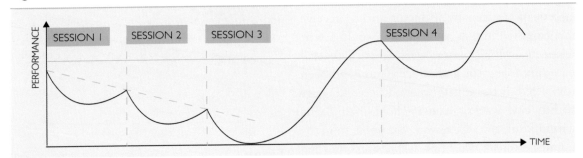

Figure 1.6 Training too soon followed by a recovery period and the correct training cycle

Figure 1.3 shows the situation for which advanced coaches strive, maximum improvement. The first training session produces the same curve as in figure 1.2, above, but then as soon as the athlete has overcompensated from the session and is at peak performance, the coach arranges another training session. The second session takes place at a time when performance is at an overcompensation stage and leads to the same cycle of exhaustion and overcompensation so that the athlete reaches an even higher level of performance. When the peaks of each session are joined together it is easy to see how, applying this method, performance continues to improve indefinitely, until old age takes a hand.

In figure 1.4, the coach has got the timing of his or her training sessions completely wrong and it is as bad as it can get. The athlete completed the first training session and is feeling exhausted. Without giving the athlete any opportunity to recover after the session, the coach schedules another session when they still feel really tired and the athlete now feels even more exhausted. The same thing happens again and now the athlete is so fatigued that he or she is barely able to get out of bed. Eventually the athlete trips over the kerb and injures themselves due to their lack of concentration resulting from their exhaustion, or they take a week off training and catch up with their sleep.

In figure 1.5 the sessions are not very well timed. The athlete completes the first training session and overcompensates and then returns back to where they started before the coach schedules the second training session again and the same thing happens. In this way the athlete never improves, but never collapses either. Instead, the athlete keeps working, but makes no progress.

In figure 1.6 the athlete completes the first training session, does not take sufficient rest time to fully recover or overcompensate, but trains again. The same thing happens twice more and eventually the athlete collapses and takes a rest for a few days, which gives him or her the time that he or she needs to recover, so that he or she can return to training while in a state of overcompensation and train again.

There are a number of ways of determining the level of performance and level of recovery of the athlete. The simplest way is to talk to him or her and find out how they feel and then try to place them on the curve that we know follows the completion of any training session.

Another, more scientific, method involves measuring a range of physiological factors, such as pulse rate or blood pressure, which will reflect the stage of recovery in order that the timing of the next training session can be calculated so as to maximise the effect of it.

There are also a range of diagrams that have been produced by psychologists to assist athletes to describe the way that they feel so that coaches can place them according to their stage of recovery.

QUESTIONS

Level 2

Q.1. It has been estimated that twice as many athletes overtrain as undertrain. How frequently should a novice athlete train in order to make serious progress?

Q.2. List and briefly explain the seven components of fitness, in a way that will be understood by an athlete.

Q.3. List and briefly explain the five principles of training, in a way that will be understood by an athlete.

Q.4. Name five lifestyle issues that are likely to have the greatest effect on the sporting performance of a young athlete.

Q.5. Draw a rough graph that reflects the effect of a single training session on the performance of an athlete.

Q.6. List the three things that an athlete must do when he or she finishes training in order to recover, so as to be ready to train again.

Level 3

Q.1. It has been estimated that twice as many athletes overtrain as undertrain. How do we know when an athlete has recovered sufficiently after training so as to be ready to train again?

Q.2. List the seven components of fitness. Define each component in simple terms and name the sport in which athletes possessing each component are most likely to be successful.

Q.3. Define the five principles of training and the ways in which you would apply these to your training of an athlete.

Q.4. Draw a rough graph that reflects the effect of a single training session on the performance of an athlete. Mark on the graph the ideal time to arrange the next training session and draw another graph that reflects the effect of the second training session on the performance of an athlete. Discuss the practical ways in which you, as a coach, can decide when the athlete has reached the ideal time for the second session.

Q.5. List factors that will assist the recovery of an athlete after training.

Q.6. What steps would you take if you discovered that one of your athletes had turned up for training when he or she had not recovered fully from his or her previous training session?

Level 4

Q.1. Explain the ways in which you would monitor and control the frequency and intensity of training for an ambitious athlete.

Q.2. Define the steps that you would take in order to increase the frequency and intensity of training for a young athlete who has been keeping fit, but who now wants to achieve sporting success.

Q.3. Set out the advice on lifestyle that you would give to a young athlete embarking on a career in competitive sport.

Q.4. An athlete has been training with you for several years, aiming at sporting success. Suddenly, he complains of constantly feeling tired and this is reflected in his sporting performances, although his training has not changed for years. Explain what you think might have happened and the way in which you might investigate further.

Q.5. At what age may people start a programme of resistance training?

Q.6. Is it possible to increase strength without increasing bodyweight? Explain how this can be achieved.

SAFETY IN WEIGHTLIFTING

0.0012

Weightlifting has been shown to be one of the safest of all sports, with an average of 0.0012 accidents for every 100 hours of participation. Considering that the sports with fewer injuries include fishing and angling, this is pretty impressive and surprises many people. The fact is that a weightlifting gymnasium is very similar to a physiotherapy studio, where people go in order to recover from injury. Both places will contain free weights, multigyms, medicine balls and wall-bars and employ professional trainers to supervise the area and give advice to those using the equipment.

In a well-run weightlifting gym, every movement performed by the athletes while training will have been carefully planned by the coach. When a coach designs a programme for one of his or her athletes, it will take into consideration the muscles that will be used, the ways in which they will be used, the weight to be used, etc. Compare that with a football match in which the coach blows his or her whistle and everybody 'dives in'. It is impossible to predict what will happen next and so much depends on the other players. Then consider rugby, and remember that when you are running around and changing directions you are likely to be hit by a 125kg prop forward, just as you turn. Is it any wonder that, in terms of hours of participation, rugby has more than 15 times the number of injuries compared to weightlifting?

However, we must not become complacent and there is always more that can be done to eliminate risks to those training in a weightlifting gym. It is when we lose our concentration that accidents happen and people start to get hurt. Due to the current era of financial cutbacks, there will always be pressure to make savings and to trim services; however, cuts below a certain level lead to accidents and injuries.

THE HISTORY OF SAFETY IN WEIGHTLIFTING

Weightlifting is a sport with a history of almost 3000 years. When it started, in Greece and Persia, it was a pastime only considered suitable for the strongest, roughest and toughest men and it involved lifting big, heavy stones, either outdoors or in caves. The activity was not organised in any way, with young men simply testing their strength, alone or with friends, probably at a local quarry where stones of a variety of sizes would have been available. The danger in lifting stones is clear for all to see. Technique had not been standardised and would have varied according to the size, shape and weight of the stone being lifted. There were no scales available to calculate the weight of each stone, so nobody knew how much weight they were attempting and even whether it was within mankind's capability. Stones tend to have sharp and rough edges and no place to grip them, so the lifters were likely to suffer multiple cuts and bruises and to drop weights that they possessed the strength to successfully lift. With temperatures in Greece and Persia being quite high, records show that they wore light clothing and usually simple sandals on their feet (clothing that was quite unsuitable for lifting weights safely).

Since those early days, weightlifting has become a sport based on strict scientific principles. These basic principles were established in ancient Greece. It was Hippocrates, the father of modern medicine, who wrote 'that which is used develops, and that which is not used wastes away.' The principles of progressive resistance training, with the need for constant overload, were established by Milo of Croton, as set out in chapter 1.

In weightlifting's infancy, men who wanted to get bigger and stronger lifted anything that they could find that suited their purpose. This might be stones or logs, the type of things that they came across in their daily lives, but as time passed, as with all things, men sought to organise their activities. In ancient Greece, the physician Galen described the use of 'halteres', a form of early dumbbell, in the second century AD. In ancient Persia there is evidence that early weightlifters used Indian clubs called 'meels'. These objects would probably have been designed so that they had smooth edges to avoid injuring the lifter,

convenient areas for gripping them, and maybe even standardised weights.

Towards the end of the 19th century there was a substantial expansion of sport that eventually lead to the formation of national governing bodies for most sports, including weightlifting, and of the International Weightlifting Federation (IWF) itself. Competitions were arranged, rules were formalised and in 1896 the International Olympic Committee (IOC) was formed and the first modern Olympic Games organised in Athens. Techniques were now established that permitted safe lifting in both training and competition, and soon books and magazines were published to circulate advice to lifters. Nowadays arrangements have got to a stage where everybody can take part using attractive, brightly coloured, carefully machined equipment in smart, centrally heated and air-conditioned gymnasia. The sport has come a long way and, as a consequence, is a great deal safer than it was in the early days.

THE USE OF WEIGHTS BY WOMEN AND CHILDREN

Historically, the use of weights by women and children has provoked considerable debate. It used to be said that women would grow bigger and more muscled if they lifted weights, but in recent years it has been shown that there is no reason they should get bulkier unless they train in a way that specifically promotes growth.

It was also thought that children would injure the epiphyseal plates at the ends of their long bones and thereby stunt their growth, lose flexibility and become muscle-bound if they lifted weights; these views received official credence when, in 1947, the Department for Education produced a paper expressing the view that it was not safe for school-age children to participate in lifting weights. In the years that followed the school leaving age was raised several times without this opinion being reviewed.

Around the end of the millennium, the sports science community across the world decided to investigate the use of weights by young people. Several countries selected committees of specialists to undertake specific research into the safety of lifting weights by young people, and gave instructions to publish their findings. In the UK, the British Association of Sports and Exercise Sciences (BASES) published its report in 2004, the *BASES Position Statement on Guidelines for Resistance Exercise in Young People*, which was produced by a committee of experts in medicine and sports science and chaired by Gareth Stratton of Liverpool John Moores University. The first recommendation in the report was that 'All young people should be encouraged to participate in safe and effective resistance exercise at least twice a week', and it went on to describe strength as 'essential for healthy living and the development of the healthy child'. The authors also recognise that resistance training may take many different forms. (Stratton et al., 2004.)

In the USA, the National Strength and Conditioning Association (NSCA) published a paper entitled *Youth Resistance Training: Position Statement Paper and Literature Review*, which stated that 'it is the current position of the NSCA that a properly designed and supervised resistance training programme is safe for children.' (Faigenbaum et al., 1996.) The Canadian Society for Exercise Physiology produced its *Position paper: Resistance training in children and adolescents* (Behm et al., 2008), which reached largely similar conclusions.

Several of the leading authors on strength training have now published books around the subject (*see* Bibliography: Fleck and Kraemer, 1993; Faigenbaum and Westcott, 2000). It is interesting to note that the person voted the best weightlifter of the 20th century and the first person to clean and jerk three times his bodyweight was a 16-year-old boy. Naim Suleymanov won Olympic gold medals in 1988, 1992 and 1996, when he was refereed by the author.

Muscular strength gains have been evident across all maturity stages, including pre-pubescents (Rians et al., 1987; Blimkie et al., 1989; Ramsay et al., 1990; Faigenbaum et al., 1993), pubescents and post-pubescents (Pfeiffer and Francis, 1986).

There is now an almost universal acceptance among sports scientists and medical professionals that resistance training is safe for all ages and both genders, and that all the identified risks of lifting weights can be significantly reduced by high-quality professional coaching. A number of high-profile, respected bodies have published policy statements on resistance training for young people which confirm these views.

HAZARDS AND RISKS

In order to discuss health and safety issues and to identify the risks associated with using weights, it is necessary to understand the basic concepts involved.

A **hazard** is something that can cause an accident or an injury. It can be anything from a cable left lying on the floor that people can trip over, to lifting a bar with weights on it, but without the collars used to secure the weights onto the bar.

A **risk** is the likelihood that the hazard will actually cause an accident or an injury. So, if the cable is in a corner of a room which is seldom used then the risk may be only 10%, but if the cable is quite taut and lying in the middle of the room then the risk might be 95%.

In order to be able to assess hazards and risks, it is essential to think creatively about situations and the problems that they may create. For this reason, a few scenarios have been designed to A) get the reader into the right frame of mind to be able to identify the issues that might give rise to concern, and to B) be able to write a rule that could be posted on a notice on the gym wall and which would prevent the problem from arising again.

SAFETY SCENARIOS

- Albert is bench pressing when all of the discs fall off one end of the bar.
- Barbara pushes a woman away from her and she knocks into somebody who is squatting.
- Charles has not been training since he broke his arm. Now he is going to have to work hard to win the championships.
- Debra has come straight from her A-level examinations and wants to de-stress.
- Edward is using the calf raise on the multigym when the weight jams, but he can see the problem and thinks that he can fix it.
- Fiona is using the lat machine when the cable snaps.
- George has just finished swimming and decides to do some weights. He didn't bring any training gear.
- Hazel has just come from work and has forgotten her training gear. She doesn't mind tearing her jeans.
- Ian has been bench pressing for years and has never had an accident. The only other people in

the gym are female and he thinks that they cannot handle heavy weights, so he decides to continue without spotters.
- Julie finds that the leg press machine has been taken out of service. But it looks OK and she only needs to do one set to complete her schedule.

Now you may wish to compare the rules that you have written with the ones that we have produced on the following pages.

Hopefully you are now even more attuned to the dangers involved in lifting heavy weights and you are ready to undertake a full safety inspection of the gymnasium that you currently use. It is hoped that the following guidance will assist you.

SAFETY INSPECTIONS

There are any number of items that need to be checked before a gymnasium may be used safely. The following is a brief summation of some of the most important ones:

Enter the room by the main entrance and walk diagonally across the room to the opposite corner. Then look back across the room and consider:

- the temperature in the gymnasium and whether it is too hot or too cold for comfort;
- the lighting in the gymnasium and whether any part of the room is receiving insufficient light for safe use;
- the background nose in the room and whether it is likely to prohibit safe and necessary communication between athletes or between athlete and trainer;
- whether there is too much equipment in the gym or in any particular part of it.

Next, move around the room and check the flooring:

- Is it flat and level?
- Are there mats or cables lying across it?
- Is the surface non-slip?

Now, check the walls and windows etc:

- How many fire exits are there?
- What are the windows and mirrors made of?
- Where is the nearest fire extinguisher? Is it suitable for electrical fires?
- Has a list of safety rules been put on the wall where it can be clearly seen?

You should also know who is in charge of the gym, and what they are doing/where they are while you are in the gym.

Finally, check each piece of apparatus:

- Look first without touching.
- Now try as if you are the user.
- Make sure that you check every piece of apparatus and that you do not miss any.

MACHINE WEIGHTS

Machines are not safer than free weights just because they are machines. There is a long history of serious accidents from weight training machinery.

However, the machines are marvellous because:

- people like to use them and they therefore encourage exercise;
- they are tidy and ready to use at all times;
- no-one steals them;
- they are quiet and don't damage the floor;
- they don't 'show up' the weaker user.

SAFE MANAGEMENT OF MACHINES

Because accidents can happen, safety guidelines must be followed.

- Supervision is necessary. Children must be continuously supervised by trained adults.
- Children need machinery which adjusts to their body size: low benches; shorter seats; lower shoulder pads.
- Moving parts must be enclosed.
- Service and repair arrangements must be assured. Ask other clients for their experience.
- Regularly inspect all moving parts (e.g. belts, pivots, slides, pulleys and sheaves).
- Regularly inspect all welds.

- Choose equipment designs which permit a full range of movement.
- Choose designs with locking pins which are unlikely to work loose.
- People forget. Reinforce your introductory user course with regular supervision.

SAFETY RULES FOR MACHINE USERS

- Adjust seat backs to ensure that the whole back is supported.
- Adjust bench heights so that your feet stabilise you by pressing on the floor, or use blocks under your feet. Do not adopt unstable bench press positions.
- Place your full shoe sole on foot plates so you cannot slip between the plate and the frame.
- Watch that your locking pins are firmly in place.
- Remember that partial movements reduce joint mobility and lead to injury.
- Use grip widths (rowing, pull-downs) which allow full movement range.
- Check that linkages are secure, cables and belts are not frayed, and cables are correctly located in pulleys.
- Keep fingers, toes and hair away from moving parts.
- Report any malfunction of machinery.
- Always choose light resistance when trying a new exercise.
- Keep warm; don't queue for long periods if a machine is busy.
- Warm up thoroughly before starting on machines (every major muscle and joint).
- Remember, if you are lying or sitting down, you cannot move quickly. Be sure that the machinery is stable.

SAFETY RULES FOR FREE WEIGHTS

Weights make no distinction between beginners and champions! They can hurt! The skills of weight training must be well learned. Poor technique, reckless additions of weight and foolish behaviour can cause accidents. Athletes need to always listen to their coach or trainer and accept advice. They should respect others' limitations and think straight before they start to train.

People say unkind things about thoughtless weight trainers who don't think and get hurt. 'Don't worry, he's all muscle, especially his head' or 'He's as strong as an ox and nearly as bright'. Yes, someone else's lack of thought might cause an injury, but if you ensure that those you train think and behave responsibly, they'll avoid hurting themselves or anyone else.

Consider the following:

- Confidence should not be confused with recklessness. The former is built on knowledge, the latter on ignorance. The only impression reckless weight training makes is on the floor.
- Although weight training and weightlifting are great fun because you can see and take pride in the progress you are making, to become an expert still takes time – time spent on understanding and mastering each stage before moving on to the next.
- Before trying new exercises or training plans and schedules, an athlete should get and follow advice from their teacher or coach, whose job it is to ensure that all the experiences that an athlete will have from the use of weights will be positive ones.
- An athlete should never train alone and should always have one spotter/stand-in at each end of the bar for squats, bench presses and fast overhead lifts. Spotters should know what the athlete is going to do and when. They should be experienced in their task.
- An athlete should keep to their schedule. They should not advance poundage without their coach's advice.
- A 'flat back' should be maintained at all times (unless otherwise instructed for certain exercises). The bar should be gripped firmly, thumbs wrapped around. Do not sacrifice correct posture for extra weight.
- Athletes should be told to not try to keep up with others who may seem to be making more rapid progress. They should train at their own level and within their own capabilities. Assure them that they will make progress.
- Horseplay and practical jokes can be very dangerous. If your athlete is not getting fun out of serious weightlifting work, it's a poor programme.
- All those in the gym should wear firm training shoes of normal construction and heel height at all times. Clothing must be warm and permit full range of movement.
- Check all apparatus before use and after each exercise. Check collars. Make sure they are firmly secured. Make sure all bars are evenly loaded. Keep the floor area tidy. Stack all loose weights when not being used. Concentrate and be safety conscious.
- When an athlete is ready for competition lifting, it will require that he or she has followed a sound training programme. Technique must be mastered. Strength and power building must be developed steadily. Success in competition will depend upon a controlled and progressive approach to training.

- No one in a gym should wear any jewellery. Rings, chains and pendants and any object with a pin can be dangerous and should always be removed while training.

SPOTTING

One of the most important safety factors when lifting heavy weights is spotting. While it is normally sufficient to be able to handle the incremental increase from the previous lift, it is occasionally necessary for a spotter to assume responsibility for the entire weight on the bar.

Spotting requires:

- strength
- footing and grip
- knowledge
- communication and co-ordination

Before agreeing to spot for a fellow gym user stop and think about what is being asked of you; it is a serious responsibility. The consequences of failure could be serious injury for all of you. Take a second to count up the weight on the bar. Ask yourself whether you can take the weight off the lifter if he or she collapses with an injury. If not, then it is better to seek more help or to decline the request.

Ask yourself where you are going to stand. Very often I have seen spotters standing next to piles of loose weights which will slip over each other if somebody stands on them. Ask yourself what you have to grab hold of when something goes wrong? I have seen bars loaded with every

spare disk in the gym so that there is no part of the bar to hold on to. Remember it is almost impossible to get a hold on a disk that will allow you to lift the bar.

A spotter needs to know everything about what is planned. We have discussed the weight on the bar, but what exercise is proposed? How many repetitions are planned? The little details also need to be discussed. Remember that lifting a heavy bar is a delicate exercise. Touch a maximum weight as it is being lifted by someone else and you can almost certainly guarantee that the lift will be failed and that the weight is likely to be dropped. Failure to catch it as it comes down will result in serious injury.

Co-ordination is therefore necessary in order to avoid touching a maximum weight un-necessarily. The lifter and the spotters need to be able to communicate with each other so as to be able to co-ordinate their actions. Remember that

In the late 1970s some of the best weightlifters, powerlifters and heavy throwers in the country trained together at the Crystal Palace National Sports Centre in south London. Every Monday, Wednesday and Friday evening a dozen of the strongest men ever to have lived in this country came together to lift heavy weights. Another 20 heavy trainers worked out in the gym at the same time and happily assisted with loading and spotting. It was a busy place.

One Friday evening the usual session was taking place. An Olympic training weekend was due to start on the Saturday and a couple of the lifters decided to finish early and go for a shower. One determined lifter resolved to stay in order to finish his planned session, but he failed to ask enough people to stay behind with him in order to ensure his safety and, one by one, the others left the gym. The lifter got to a point where he was squatting 365kg for a set of three repetitions and he was in the gym with a couple of stragglers. As he went down for his final repetition his knee locked, and he could not move it. He was sitting in a full squat with 365kg on his back. He was unable to get up or to move without injuring himself further. All that he could do was stay where he was. To have unloaded the disks from the bar would have caused movement that was likely to injure his knee even more severely.

An ambulance was called and arrived within a few minutes, but when the paramedics arrived they could do nothing. Meanwhile, a lifter had been found in the next room on some light weights and he rushed around the showers summoning the other weightlifters, powerlifters and throwers back to the gym. They quickly dried and dressed themselves and ran back to help. By now several minutes had passed.

The area around the lifter had to be cleared of weights in order to provide a foothold for the spotters. A grip had to be secured onto a heavily loaded bar. Despite their great combined strength it was extremely difficult for these men to lift the bar, as 10 men trying to find somewhere to stand and somewhere to grip a fully-laden bar could generate little force, but eventually they managed to remove the bar from the lifter and allow the ambulance crew to take him to hospital. By the time that the lifter was taken to hospital it was estimated that he had been sitting in the full squat position with 800lbs on his back for 15 minutes.

there may be a lot of noise in a busy gym and that everybody must be able to make themselves heard, so there is no room for shrinking violets. Shout if you have to. Ask for loud music to be turned down if you need peace and quiet in order to ensure safety.

As has been mentioned, weightlifting is a very safe sport, with fewer accidents than almost every other sport, but accidents do happen, as they will in any activity. The author has almost 40 years' experience of working regularly in gymnasia around the world and has only witnessed two or three serious accidents in that time. However, the most serious accident that he has seen reflects many of the problems that can occur when things go wrong.

LOADING
THE START OF THE SESSION

The decision as to what weight to load onto a weightlifting bar is as important as any in the sport. Clearly, the weight on the bar is integral to whether the lift is successful or not, and there is little benefit in a failed lift.

Successful lifts breed confidence: self-confidence for the lifter, but also confidence from the lifter in the coach and in his or her judgement, which may be vital in a competitive situation. Failed lifts mean weights falling to the floor – with the associated risk of injury to the lifter, the coach or other lifters and of damage to the gymnasium and the equipment in it. While it is impossible to eliminate all failure from the gym, the proportion of failures should be low and training programmes need to be designed with this in mind.

The principles of warming up apply to the lifting of weights as much as they do in every other sport. At the start of every session, an athlete needs to warm up in order to prepare to lift heavy weights and to reduce the risk of injury. The three objectives of a warm up programme are:

1. To raise body temperature by 1°C by some form of aerobic exercise that increases heart rate, blood flow and therefore circulation;
2. To stretch the muscles so that they are allowing a free range of movement;
3. To mentally prepare for the activities that are about to take place.

Some lifters, particularly in the early stages of their career, will undertake a little skipping or light jogging in order to increase their circulation. They will then do a little gentle stretching with some arm circling, some deep squatting, some wrist and ankle stretches. It is at about this time that many lifters start to become quiet as they start to focus on the forthcoming session and what they have to do. They will start to run through mental preparations for the movements that they are to perform. For example, an athlete capable of snatching 200kg may snatch with an empty bar in order to rehearse the movement, and to complete the stretching by sitting deep in the squat snatch position and then pushing one knee out and then the other knee, or twisting so as to stretch one shoulder then the other.

The lifter will usually do two sets with the empty bar in this way before putting a 15kg disc on each end of the bar (to give him a total of 50kg) and doing two more sets. It is now time to put a 20kg disc on each end of the bar (to give him a total of 90kg) and start snatching quickly in order to focus on the speed required in snatching, but it should be remembered that, despite having completed five sets of snatches, the lifter is still performing at only 45% of his personal best. Typical progression from this point may then involve adding 10kg discs on each side to give 110kg, then 130kg and 150kg, so that the lifter will have completed eight sets by the time that he has reached 75% of his best.

Now the warm-up is complete and the actual serious lifting starts; progression will be reduced to 10kg then 5kg on a general training day, and to 2kg and 1kg on a day for maximums.

THE END OF THE SESSION

Clearly the lifting of heavy weights is designed to improve strength and, having completed the warm-up, it is time to focus on improving strength. Those lifters whose entire focus is on becoming strong do not need to consider lifting weights for more than six repetitions, unless specifically attempting to improve fitness. Rowers and others who need to combine strength and endurance will need to consider sets of as many as 20 repetitions in order to achieve this.

Training programmes tend to be set out in a number of ways:

Sets. This is where the hard work necessary to make progress is done. A lifter may undertake something like six sets of six repetitions for six weeks during the out-of-competition phase of training. The lifter gets stronger as a result of this hard work, but this is not reflected by an increase in poundages due to exhaustion from all the hard work.

Pyramids. In this system the lifter starts with a broad base of six repetitions, but then reduces it to four, three, two and one repetitions in the following sets. A pyramid often follows a period of sets and as a result of less work and greater recovery, this is where the increases in poundages will be realised.

Maximums. In some places, where athletes are training six days a week and sometimes twice a day, it is customary to set one day each week aside to attack maximum poundages. As well as ensuring that there is an accurate assessment of the maximum weight that each athlete can lift in each exercise, it also puts the athlete under the same physical, physiological and psychological pressure that they will have to handle in competition. After a thorough warm-up, the lifter quickly moves through a few sets of three repetitions and two repetitions and then works on single lifts until they fail a lift.

When lifting sets of repetitions then the poundages will differ little from day to day. Even when undertaking hard training in order to make improvements, progress is slow and lifters should only expect to improve by 1kg or 2kg at a time; attempts at greater poundage are pointless. The ambition should be slow, steady progress made relentlessly over a number of years, rather than spectacular improvements made over a short period of time.

When an athlete makes spectacular progress over a short length of time then he or she is likely to attract attention from drug control officers who are more worried about how this is being achieved, rather than being impressed at the speed of the progress.

GENERAL HEALTH AND SAFETY ADVICE

Over recent years there has been a focus on improving health and safety with the intention of reducing the number and severity of accidents that occur. The following general advice applies equally to all business or community facilities, whatever their use.

All premises should have adequate first-aid equipment and sufficient qualified first-aiders to deal with any likely emergency on the premises. Where the premises are opened for extended hours then steps should be taken to ensure that the first-aiders are organised to cover the hours when the premises are open and operating.

Adequate fire exits to allow those on the premises to escape in the case of fire or other emergency should be available, regularly checked for ease of operation and access should be clearly marked and illuminated. Fire marshals should be appointed who have been trained in their duties and provided with the necessary clothing to identify them in case of emergency. Fire extinguishers of sufficient number and of an appropriate design for the likely risks should be readily available, clearly marked and regularly tested.

Telephones providing access to the public telephone system must be available so that calls may be made to the emergency services in cases of accident or injury. If these telephones are mobile rather then landlines then arrangements must be made to ensure sufficient signal, credit and battery life so that calls may be made when necessary. In addition, all the telephone numbers that may be required must be available and regularly checked. These will include the numbers of the emergency services and the home numbers and next of kin numbers for all members using the centre, particularly those who are young people or those with a disability or special medical needs.

SUMMARY

The main reason why weight training is so safe is that the coach is able to give instructions on the exercise to be performed, the weight to be used, the style to be adopted and in this way is determining which muscles will be used, in which order and the amount of effort expended. Everything is controlled.

Accidents can happen in weight training, but they can nearly all be prevented by proper coaching and attention to detail. Equipment needs to be checked, and when it is properly looked after then problems can be dealt with before accidents even occur.

Discipline must be maintained in every gymnasium. That does not mean that people must be miserable and/or silent. It means that people must behave sensibly and observe proper procedures. When correct techniques and proper procedures have been learnt then trainers can enjoy a laugh and a joke, provided that standards are maintained. We all want people to enjoy themselves and come again.

A coach should reiterate that fun comes from seeing the progress that an athlete and their friends are making and from the friendships that can be forged by regular training. It can only be spoilt by accidents and friends being hurt.

All weightlifters, no matter how experienced should get and follow good advice from a coach!

WHAT TO DO WHEN AN ACCIDENT OCCURS

There is no way to entirely eliminate the risk of accidents, whatever precautions are taken, so we must now discuss the steps to take when an accident occurs.

REPORTING AND RECORDING ACCIDENTS

- All relevant information must be recorded.
- With most people now possessing mobile phones with cameras, it makes sense to photograph the scene of any accident.
- Accidents must be reported to the responsible authority and recorded.

- All communications and records must be clear and accurate.

EMERGENCY PROCEDURES

- Procedures laid down must be consistent with approved practice and must be accurately followed when an emergency arises.
- The location of information relevant to emergency procedures and equipment must be communicated clearly to participants and any others with whom the instructor has contact.
- Ensure that information required to contact others in an emergency is readily available.
- Co-operate fully with any emergency drills laid down for the training area or establishment.
- In the event of an emergency, procedures must be carried out promptly, accurately and calmly.
- All incidents must be reported promptly and recorded accurately.

Remember!

It is too late to find out what to do and where to find emergency exits when an accident occurs. It is your job to research these things and to know the answers before you start working. It may save a life!

QUESTIONS

Level 2

Q.1. Describe how you would prepare for a weights class so as to ensure the safety of those taking part.

Q.2. List the rules that you would set down in respect of the clothing to be worn by participants when you are in charge of the gym.

Q.3. List the rules that you would set down in respect of the behaviour of participants when you are in charge of the gym.

Q.4. List 10 questions that you would want to have answered by participants before allowing them to join a class that you were teaching in the gym.

Q.5. Why is it so dangerous to train alone in a gym?

Q.6. Set out the steps that you would take at the end of a session that you are coaching.

Level 3

Q.1. As part of a safety inspection of the gym you discover that a piece of equipment is defective. Set out the action that you would take to deal with the issue.

Q.2. A young athlete who you are coaching, and who you believe has a bright future in strength sport, is reluctant to commit as he believes that weights are dangerous. Set out the argument that you would use to convince him that weights are safe.

Q.3. The father of a young athlete that you coach turns up at the gym and tells you that he has been told by friends that weights are not safe for those under 18 years of age. Set out the argument that you would use to convince him that weights are safe for everybody.

Q.4. What steps could you take to show your clients how committed you are to health and safety?

Q.5. Set out the arrangements that you would make for spotters during an attempt at the world record for the bench press. List the instructions that you would give them in order to ensure the safety of all concerned. What is the heaviest weight that might be used and how many spotters would you need for that weight?

Q.6. When lifting 80% or more of personal best poundage, what would be the usual maximum increase between attempts?

Level 4

Q.1. Describe the method used to inspect a gym for safety.

Q.2. Explain the difference between a hazard and a risk in health and safety legislation.

Q.3. The father of a young athlete that you coach turns up at the gym and tells you that he has been told by friends that weights are not safe for those under 18 years of age. You set out your case, but he continues to express doubts. What books or papers could you refer him to in support of your argument?

Q.4. Set out the arrangements that you would make for spotters during an attempt at the world record for the back squat. List the instructions that you would give them in order to ensure the safety of all concerned. What is the heaviest weight that might be used and how many spotters would you need for that weight?

Q.5. Set out the procedures to be followed when all else fails and an accident occurs.

Q.6. Safety is more important than customer satisfaction and customer satisfaction will not last long if people are injured in the gym. Discuss.

DRUGS

> It must be noted that the comments and advice given here are general and not specific to any one sport or testing agency. This chapter needs to be read in conjunction with the most recent doping regulations of the sport concerned and of the competition entered.

As science and medicine continue their relentless advance, and work and business consume more and more of our time, it is becoming more usual for us to look towards pills and medicine to improve our health and lifestyle.

Many people rush to the medicine cabinet as their first response to any problem and taking pills has become commonplace. As a sports coach, I became aware of a married couple who were taking 25 vitamin tablets a day each and they enjoyed a feast of pills every morning. Soon they were skipping breakfast in order to take the pills and frequently their stomachs rejected the pills and they were physically sick. And they did this to improve their health and fitness?

A senior consultant physician, recognising that I was losing my hair, offered to prescribe a cardiac medication that I could take on a daily basis for the rest of my life, to stop the hair loss. This is clearly a disproportionate reaction to an insignificant problem, but it reflects society's view that every problem has a cure in pill form.

DRUGS IN SPORT

It has often been said that 'sport reflects society' and it certainly does in respect to drugs. Sport plays a vital role in modern life, with many people starting their day by reading the back pages of the newspaper over the breakfast table. Success in sport results in financial success, with businesses queuing up to sign sponsorship deals with successful teams and leading individual players and athletes. Failure leads to decreased or removed financial backing, lowered earning potential or even dismissal.

When the modern Olympics were established in 1896 there is evidence that drugs such as arsenic and strychnine were taken in order to improve performance. The modern Olympics required athletes to be selected by their national governing body and their national Olympic committee and to compete wearing national uniform under a national flag. It is hardly surprising, therefore, that after initial reluctance, Adolf Hitler and the National Socialist Party took such a great interest in organising the 1936 Olympic Games in Berlin.

After the Second World War, in 1945, Germany was divided into two republics. West Germany was initially controlled by the USA, Britain and France and was by far the larger. East Germany was initially controlled by the Soviet Union and was much smaller, but was considerably more successful at sport. The reason for the East German success was that the leaders decided to use success at sport as a way to demonstrate the success of their political system, and decided to invest a considerable amount of time and money in developing sport science.

There is also clear evidence that many elite and developing athletes, irrespective of age or gender, were supplied with the drugs necessary to improve sporting performance, and that the East Germans set up organisations to ruthlessly exploit drugs by researching the best ways to use them and to infiltrate even the Olympic movement, in order to sabotage the testing procedures and therefore reduce the risk of detection for their athletes.

It was in the immediate post-war years that the drugs which we all think of when doping in sport is discussed started to be used by athletes. Anabolic steroids, which are synthetic copies of the male hormone testosterone, were discovered in the 1930s and during the Second World War there is evidence that their use was investigated as a way to improve the fighting qualities of soldiers. Put simply, they will stimulate an increase of the male characteristics such as increasing bodyweight and muscle mass, increasing aggression, promoting hair growth and deepening the voice.

During the 1950s and 1960s there was a whispering campaign in sporting circles and in the press that drugs were increasingly involved in sport. This was during the Cold War, the stand-off between the USA and the Soviet Union and, as one might expect in these circumstances, the Western media focused allegations of drug abuse against the Soviet athletes, such as the Press sisters.

Sisters Tamara and Irina Press were both Olympic champions for the Soviet Union in the early 1960s. Western track and field officials and media representatives often mocked the muscular sisters for appearing masculine, and speculated, whether fairly or not, that the two received male hormone treatments, or perhaps were actually men. In part because of those questions, gender tests were instituted for international competitions in 1966. The sisters promptly withdrew from athletic competition and were never tested, fueling further speculation. Soviet officials announced the pair were retiring to care for their ailing mother in Ukraine.

The effects of anabolic steroids although powerful, are not spectacular, and with the world recovering from the Second World War, stamping out doping in sport was not seen as a priority. In fact, it was not anabolic steroids but another type of drug, stimulants, that eventually prompted the authorities to take action against drugs in sport. The slow, painful death of British cyclist Tommy Simpson during the 1967 Tour de France, broadcast live on the emerging technology of television, shocked the world into action (while the facts are not totally clear, Simpson's consumption of stimulants were a factor in his death).

Research to identify forensic tests to provide evidence of drug use and the political negotiations necessary to set up the structures to introduce and manage the testing took almost 14 years, with the testing programmes finally being introduced in 1981.

As with all new procedures, the testing took time to become established. The first positive cases provoked legal challenges until a consensus was reached and the new rules become embedded. The initial difficulty in securing the anticipated level of positive results in relation to anabolic steroids reminded those carrying out the tests that, unlike stimulants, anabolic steroids do not need to be taken at or around the time of the competition in order to be effective. It is very easy for athletes to take anabolic steroids during their off season preparations and then stop taking them as the competitive season approaches. It was for this reason that the testers then decided to change their focus to out-of-competition testing and to require athletes from all sports to lodge details of their accommodation and training so that they could be quickly traced for an out-of-competition drugs test, which have, over time, proved more successful in identifying those using anabolic steroids.

The most recent development in drugs in sport is the use of anabolic steroids by young men and women who do not participate in competitive sport, but who simply want to look attractive to their friends and partners. Many of these people do not even undertake any sports or fitness training and simply rely on the anabolic steroids to improve their appearance. Closely linked to this is the use of anabolic steroids by men and women working as doormen or 'door executives' (bouncers), in charge of security at nightclubs, pubs and restaurants, who feel the need to feel big, 'pumped' and aggressive in order to confront those with whom they have to deal in potentially violent situations.

FITNESS INSTRUCTORS, PERSONAL TRAINERS AND WEIGHTLIFTING COACHES

If anabolic steroids are the most popular drugs used in sport and they make you bigger and stronger, it is not surprising that the first place that many people, including investigative journalists, go to find out about anabolic steroids, what they do and where to get them, is the gym.

Few fitness instructors working in gymnasia across the country have not been asked about drugs in general and anabolic steroids in particular. It is no longer acceptable to brush these questions off with a few, well-chosen platitudes and today it falls to those people working in the fitness industry to provide the essential information needed by people who may consider using drugs in order to improve their appearance, performance or fitness.

Just as society has accepted that young people must be informed about the consequences of sexual activity, then they must be informed about using drugs, including their effects on performance, the likely side effects, testing and detection methods and the consequences of conviction. If it is not possible to secure the latest scientific information relating to the use of drugs in sport, it cannot be surprising that people are making bad decisions on the subject.

This book is entitled the *Complete Guide to Lifting Heavy Weights* and it certainly could not claim to be that nowadays if it did not cover the use of drugs in sport.

THE WORLD ANTI-DOPING AGENCY (WADA)

The world of sport is traditionally led by the International Olympic Committee (IOC) and its Medical Committee led the fight against doping until 1999, when WADA was formed.

THE PROHIBITED LIST

WADA knows that some athletes take substances and employ methods in order to gain an unfair advantage over their rivals. It has consulted widely with doctors, scientists, coaches and athletes and produced a list of these substances and methods, which is called the *Prohibited List*. The list is updated every year, with more frequent updates in cases of special need.

Participation in sporting events is generally subject to participants agreeing to refrain from employing these substances and methods, and submitting themselves to a range of detection methods.

WADA works closely with the IOC, international federations of sport and national governing bodies of sport. In recent years, WADA has been building links with national governments and law enforcement agencies and encouraging these bodies to co-operate with them in detecting drugs offences by athletes.

In the UK, as in most countries, it is necessary to prove that a person guilty of a crime has a guilty mind (*mens rea*) as well as the fact that he or she has committed a guilty act (*actus reas*). This means that in order to be found guilty in a criminal court of possessing a controlled drug such as heroin, then there must be evidence that the person knew that there was powder in the pocket, that it was heroin and that possessing heroin was against the law.

WADA employs the principles of strict liability, which for example means that when a prohibited substance is found in an athlete's pocket, then there is a presumption that the athlete knew that it was there, knew that it was prohibited and knew that it was an offence to possess it.

Many athletes who have been found to have taken substances/used methods on the *Prohibited List* have produced team doctors to say that they prescribed the substance/method to the athlete in order to treat a genuine medical problem. The principle of strict liability means that this does not excuse the athlete, who must take personal responsibility for checking any substance that he or she takes before using it.

Only if the athlete will suffer health consequences as a result of not taking the substance may it be taken, and this must then be reported to the relevant testing agencies and sporting bodies as soon as practicable. The use of the substance or method will then disqualify the athlete from future participation in sport for a period to be determined by the testing and sporting authorities so as to allow the substance or the effects of the method to clear the athlete's system. This can only be avoided by securing a therapeutic use exemption (*see* opposite).

WADA's regulations also contain catch-all clauses and rules in order to permit action against people who attempt to defeat the spirit of the regulations by possessing or using substances and methods which are similar to items on the *Prohibited List*, but which may not be listed yet.

The 2010 list consists of:

S1. Anabolic agents
S2. Peptide hormones, growth factors and related substances
S3. Beta-2 agonists
S4. Hormone antagonists and modulators
S5. Diuretics and other masking agents

In addition to the categories S1 to S5 defined above, the following categories are prohibited in competition:

S6. Stimulants
S7. Narcotics
S8. Cannabinoids
S9. Glucocorticosteroids

Substances prohibited in particular sports:

P1. Alcohol
P2. Beta-blockers

Prohibited methods are:

M1. Enhancement of oxygen transfer
M2. Chemical and physical manipulation
M3. Gene doping

THERAPEUTIC USE EXEMPTION (TUE)

Athletes will generally be fit and healthy individuals who are able to live without the assistance of medications. In fact, when people become athletes they become much more aware of their bodies and the ways in which they are working. As athletes reach international standard and secure funding to assist them to focus on their training, many give up working, which means that they have a great deal more time on their hands and focus even more on the ways that their bodies are feeling.

When the testing programme started there was a presumption that fit and healthy athletes would not need to take medication and that an athlete who needed to take medication would not subsequently compete until the medication had cleared his or her system. The welcome expansion of the Paralympics and disabled people's participation in sport generally has meant that this attitude has had to be reviewed and adapted to current circumstances. Paralympic athletes may well possess a range of health problems that require them to take regular medication out of necessity. Nowadays, an athlete advised to take medication for health reasons should notify his or her national governing body as well as the UK anti doping (UKAD), the national anti-doping agency at the earliest opportunity. If the athlete wants to continue competing then he or she may make application for a TUE by supplying all the relevant information and the name of the doctor advising the course of treatment. If the athlete intends to stop training in order to recover then he or she may take the medication and the testing authorities are informed.

BANNED SUBSTANCES
S1, S2, S3, S4, S5 AND S9.

To a non-chemist these are basically anabolic steroids and related compounds. They are hormones designed to mimic the effect on the human body of the hormone testosterone. The effects of anabolic steroids are to make people more masculine than they previously were. The effects fall into two types, the anabolic effect and the androgenic effect.

The word 'anabolic' means building and refers to the muscle- and weight-building effects. Anabolic steroids tend to increase lean muscle mass. If these drugs are taken by people who are not exercising then the effects are minimal, but if they are taken by people who are undertaking heavy training then they will speed up recovery substantially and promote considerable growth. It is for this reason that anabolic steroids are popular with athletes.

Scientists take great care when performing research in order to act ethically. Ethically, it is not acceptable to give drugs that may have negative or undetermined side effects to people who do not need them. This makes research difficult.

The androgenic effect is the masculinising effect of anabolic steroids. Athletes like the fact that it makes them feel more aggressive so that they can train harder and therefore make gains that way. The anabolic steroids also make them more hairy and give them deeper voices, which although not generally desirable in women, may be a risk that some are prepared to take.

The balance of anabolic and androgenic effects varies from drug to drug and experiences of dealing with positive drug findings indicate that athletes seek out the exact balance that they need to improve their performance in their chosen sport.

For example, an athlete in a weight-controlled sport, who is reluctant to move to a higher category, but who is keen to become more aggressive in competition, may choose to take an anabolic steroid with a high androgenic effect and a low anabolic effect.

Side effects of steroids include visible clues such as puffy cheeks, which makes users appear as if they have put on more weight than they have, and spotty backs caused by acne across the shoulders. These symptoms are a clear giveaway to the other people at the gym, who either see them in the showers or notice that they have started going home smelly instead...

There are health risks associated with long-term use or excessive doses of anabolic steroids. These effects include harmful changes in cholesterol levels (increased low-density lipoprotein and decreased high-density lipoprotein), acne, high blood pressure, liver damage (mainly with oral steroids), and dangerous changes in the structure of the left ventricle of the heart.

GROWTH HORMONE

In recent years there has been an increase in the use of growth hormone by athletes. This has been encouraged by the difficulty in identifying a satisfactory test for it, with the tests used relying on either collecting a blood sample or only being effective for the first few hours after testing. The requirement to collect a blood sample meant additional training for the sampling officers, who were more used to collecting urine samples and raised health and safety issues at a time of increased awareness surrounding transmission of HIV.

With some athletes dehydrating in order to make their weight requirement or sweating profusely during competition, sampling may make some time. Athletes who had recently injected growth hormone would take advantage of this excuse and delay providing a sample until the risk of detection had passed.

There are ethical problems with taking growth hormone that go beyond those in most other substances on the *Prohibited List*. Firstly, there is insufficient growth hormone in the world to treat all the children suffering from dwarfism as a result of a lack of it, which means that athletes taking it are depriving children of the treatment that they need. Secondly, partly as a consequence of this, much of the growth hormone available to athletes is of veterinary origin, from monkeys or cattle, with the associated risk of side effects and contamination.

The limited supply of growth hormone has restricted the research into side effects as the available growth hormone is supposed to be prescribed only to the children who need it, but it is significant that supplies of growth hormone have been found in the possessions of athletes who have been found dead while participating in sporting events.

S5. DIURETICS AND OTHER MASKING AGENTS

Diuretics increase the excretion of water from the body, although each class does so in a distinct way. When diuretics were originally banned, the reason given was because they allowed athletes in weight-controlled sports to reduce their bodyweight to unnatural levels. This is a weak argument because other substances, such as orange juice and red wine, and other methods, such as taking saunas or exercising while wrapped up in black plastic bags, have very similar effects.

The inclusion of diuretics with 'other masking agents' confirms that the real reason for banning diuretics is that they can assist in concealing the taking of anabolic steroids. A technique was developed called 'diuretic flushing' in which an athlete anticipated being tested for drugs by taking a diuretic. This caused him or her to go to the toilet and empty their bladder. The athlete then would drink some water and the bladder would re-fill with pure water. When the athlete was summoned to take a urine test in order to detect the presence of any banned substances he or she would take another diuretic tablet surreptitiously and was then able to urinate again. The sample of urine provided to the testing officer was invariably pure water without the contamination of the drugs previously taken. The water went through the intestinal system very quickly and legend had it that it was sufficiently pure for the scientists to even be able to identify the brand of the mineral water consumed!

S6. STIMULANTS

There is little to say about stimulants, as their benefits to athletes are clear for all to see. Stimulants have a short-term effect so that they have to be taken immediately before or during a competition and are therefore detected by competition testing.

An additional issue with stimulants is that many of them, such as amphetamines, are social drugs that come within the provisions of the Misuse of Drugs Act 1971, so that possession and supply are criminal offences and this, including evidence of a positive doping test, must be reported to police. Many sports administrators have found themselves at risk of criminal prosecution for failing to report a positive drug test result in respect of an athlete to the police.

S7. NARCOTICS

Many people are now in the habit of taking painkillers to deal with any discomfort. While most headache tablets are not on the banned list, some are, and every athlete must know the difference or take steps to find out with certainty.

Athletes are at a heightened risk due to the fact that they undertake regular foreign travel and therefore find themselves dealing with a wider range of drugs abroad and because they often have

doctors, nurses and other medical staff readily to hand to assist with any problem. If these staff do not know the rules, they can get themselves and their athletes into a great deal of difficulty.

Narcotics are banned to prevent athletes competing while seriously injured and therefore causing themselves even greater injury, by taking tablets or injections in order to control the pain.

S8. CANNABINOIDS

These are all the various forms of cannabis. It is a relatively mild stimulant and can improve performance. It is also a criminal offence and the comments under 'stimulants' above apply.

P1. ALCOHOL

Alcohol usually means the common alcoholic beverages that people drink in pubs, clubs or at home, but also includes any extremes such as medicinal alcohol or shoe polish.

P2. BETA-BLOCKERS

Beta-blockers are usually taken by older people with heart problems. These and alcohol are thought of in the same category because they were added to the *Prohibited List* in order to prevent target shooters gaining an unfair advantage.

The following substances/methods are limited to a few sports and for competition testing only.

M1. ENHANCEMENT OF OXYGEN TRANSFER

This was added to the *Prohibited List* when it was commented that at the time there were five ways to enhance oxygen uptake and only one of them was banned. Erythropoietin (EPO) is a glycoprotein hormone that controls erythropoiesis, or red blood cell production. Being born, or living, at high altitude has a very similar physiological effect, but is entirely natural, which means that those Ethiopian and Kenyan runners born at very high altitude have a distinct advantage over the rest of us who were born at, or close to, sea level.

Another way to secure the same effect is to sleep in an environmental chamber with restricted oxygen every night (hypoxia). These two latter enhancements were not prohibited. As there are no recorded ill effects from taking EPO there were no obvious reasons for the distinction of including only one of the methods on the *Prohibited List*.

On 21 April, 2002, the *Times* praised the England footballer David Beckham for using an environmental chamber with restricted oxygen supply to assist his recovery following injury to a bone in his left foot. The newspaper was delighted by his use of an innovative strategy designed to promote his recovery from an injury that threatened his participation in the forthcoming World Cup. It is unclear whether this support would have continued to the same degree if Beckham had been suspended for breaching the rules of the *Prohibited List*.

M2. CHEMICAL AND PHYSICAL MANIPULATION

The current prohibited list for group S2 peptide hormones, growth factors and related substances concludes with the words 'and other substances with similar chemical structure or similar biological effect(s)'. Previous versions of the *Prohibited List* finished each of the groups with a similar statement in order to avoid athletes escaping detection by adapting the substance or method is some slight way in order to bypass the regulations.

This regulation allows those enforcing the rules to take action against those clearly attempting to circumvent the regulations with some fancy scientific trick.

M3. GENE DOPING

WADA, aware that a number of athletes have been supported by state-of-the-art scientific research, is trying to get ahead of the game with this regulation. Research into genetics has been prolific and every day further research is being published. This regulation allows WADA to take action against any athlete found to have applied the latest scientific research in order to improve his or her results, possibly even before that research was published to the scientific community.

Clearly, some form of gene doping will become possible in the coming years and if this provides athletes with an opportunity to improve their performance, somebody will take advantage of it. This regulation means that if WADA find out later that this has happened and develop the technology to detect it and secure the evidence to prove it, then action may be taken.

FUTURE WADA POLICY

WADA has announced that it intends to encourage national governments to implement legislation in all countries to control the misuse of the substances used in doping in sport. It is their policy to work in co-operation with the law enforcement agencies of all national governments, such as police, customs and revenue, border agencies, coastguard and homeland security in order to detect and punish offenders.

In pursuit of this policy, WADA and the national anti-doping organisations have employed former intelligence officers in order to set up systems that will work with the aforementioned agencies and allow a high level of co-operation.

This new policy will mean that, in addition to the current practice of competition and out-of-competition testing, WADA will now encourage luggage searches, home searches, gym searches and the questioning of suspects and the use of witness evidence and admissions under caution, as evidence.

PRACTICE AND PROCEDURE

Athletes in most sports who are competing at a national level are likely to be included on a testing register and be eligible for testing both at competition and out-of-competition. While signing up to the register may well be compulsory in order to continue competing at some sports and it is ethically the right thing to do, it is still a major step to take and an athlete should read all the available literature on the subject.

Membership of the register places a number of responsibilities on the athlete to live his or her life in a disciplined manner. The athlete will have to register their place of address, place and times of training, etc, and any variations from these will have to be notified. Many athletes have been selected for competitions abroad or to participate in training camps organised by their national governing bodies, only to find that they have left frustrated sampling officers in their wake and are facing disciplinary action from the same national governing body that invited them to go to the competition or training camp.

Every out-of-competition testing register has an administrator that the athlete will have to keep

in touch with, possibly at short notice. The ready access to telephone, text messages and email provided by modern mobile phones allows athletes to maintain contact with the administrators of these registers regarding short-term emergencies that cause them to break their usual schedules.

IF YOU NEED TO FIND OUT ABOUT A DRUG THAT YOU NEED TO TAKE

Careful consideration needs to be taken by the athlete before taking any medication. The fact that the medication was recommended by a medical practitioner does not, in itself, provide any protection from the doping regulations, although it is recognised that a patient in an emergency room has little choice but to comply with doctors.

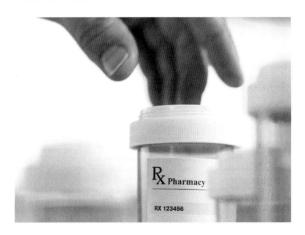

The UK Sport website (www.uksport.gov.uk) provides the best advice on all medications and whether they are on the WADA *Prohibited List* or not. Proprietary brand names of all medications available legally in the UK are shown on the website, which may be checked directly or by way of telephone. If the medication was purchased overseas or does not appear on the website then the athlete will need to find the list of ingredients and check each of these on the website individually.

If any of this seems like too much effort for an athlete in your care, tell them to remember that a positive test can result in being branded as a cheat in front of friends, suspension from further participation from their sport and may even finish up with their picture on the front page of newspapers or on television. All of this will cause pain to them and their family.

If the medication that has been recommended is on the list then the athlete should speak to their doctor and see whether there is an alternative that is equally effective but which is not on the list.

If there is no alternative to taking a medication on the *Prohibited List* then the athlete should, if possible, contact the testing authorities quickly before taking the medication, in order to avoid any possible health problems. This should only mean a two-minute delay in taking the medication. If this delay could involve risk to the athlete's health then the athlete should take the medication and inform the testing authorities at the first opportunity.

In some cases, such as with asthma, an athlete is advised by a doctor to take medication when he or she suffers an attack. Many asthma medications are on the list, so as soon as the athlete is given the advice to use the medication they should check if it is prohibited. If it is, they should find out whether there is an alternative medication which could be used, and if not then contact the testing authorities in order to apply for a therapeutic use exemption. This is the certificate granted by the testing authorities accepting that the use of the medication is essential, that there is no practical alternative and that the athlete has been exempted from the regulations and may use the medication for a prescribed period. The athlete will have to then re-apply for an extension of this TUE when it expires and there have been cases where athletes have been disciplined for failing to re-apply.

A cautionary tale is the situation that involved the British skier, Alain Baxter. In 2002 Baxter made Olympic history by becoming the first Briton to win a medal at the Winter Olympics, when he won a bronze in the alpine skiing event at Salt Lake City. A few days after his return home, Alain discovered that he had failed a drug test. His sample contained a trace amount of methamphetamine. After an appeal, the IOC declared that Baxter was disqualified from the competition and he would have to return his medal. Baxter was able to confirm later that the trace had originated from a Vicks inhaler bought in the USA. He had been unaware that the contents were different from those found in the UK version. Although the International Ski Federation accepted his explanation and banned him for the minimum of three months, his medal was not returned.

TESTING ADVICE TO ATHLETES FROM UK ANTI-DOPING (UKAD)

The testing programme is designed to protect the reputation of doping-free athletes. It is essential that athletes have confidence in the programme and understand its value as well as understanding what they can expect if they are tested.

UNDERSTANDING SAMPLE COLLECTION

- Know the sport's anti-doping regulations.

- Know the sample collection procedures and the athlete rights and responsibilities.
- Athletes should keep a list of medications, substances and supplements they take so they can accurately record them on the sample collection form at the time of testing.
- Keep a copy of the sample collection form when tested.
- Athletes on the national registered testing pool (NRTP) should maintain their athlete whereabouts filings and be available for out-of-competition testing.

TIPS FOR ATHLETES

- When notified of a test, the athlete should stay in full view of the chaperone/doping control officer (DCO)/ blood collection officer (BCO) at all times.
- Always carry photographic identification for the purpose of notification.
- Athletes are encouraged to report to the doping control station immediately.
- Athletes that do not understand the sample collection procedures should ask the DCO to explain them.

ATHLETE RIGHTS

Athletes have the right to the following:

- The DCO must have official identification and evidence of his/her authority to carry out the test from an official anti-doping organisation.
- The DCO should offer the athlete the right to be accompanied by a representative of their choice to the doping control station.
- The DCO (or witnessing official) observing the provision of the sample must be the same gender as the athlete.

- To comment on the testing procedures for each test.
- To receive a copy of the sample collection form after the test.
- To ensure confidentiality, that no name should be on any documentation intended for the laboratory.

INFORMATION FROM UKAD FOR THOSE NEW TO ELITE SPORT

Athletes have the right to compete in doping-free sport and have a responsibility to ensure they are competing without the use of prohibited substances or methods. Strict liability is a fundamental principle; athletes will be held personally responsible for any prohibited substance found in their system, regardless of how it got there.

Athletes new to elite sport need to make sure they are fully aware of their anti-doping responsibilities. The Athlete Zone of the UK Anti-Doping website should answer most questions, but below is a short summary of the key elements of anti-doping.

WORLD ANTI-DOPING CODE AND THE FIVE INTERNATIONAL STANDARDS

The World Anti-Doping Code seeks to harmonise the rules, policies and regulations regarding anti-doping across all sports and all countries. The Code is supported by five International Standards that ensure a uniformed approach to anti-doping around the world. Visit www.wada-ama.org and the World Anti-Doping Agency section of the website for more information.

TESTING AND THE NATIONAL REGISTERED TESTING POOL (NRTP)

Athletes subject to the anti-doping rules of their sport are eligible for testing at any time. In addition to this, some athletes may be selected for the National Registered Testing Pool (NRTP).

Athletes nominated for inclusion in the NRTP will be notified by their national governing body (NGB) or by UK Anti-Doping and will be required to supply details of their whereabouts for out-of-competition testing.

WHEREABOUTS

If an athlete is nominated by UK Anti-Doping or their NGB for out-of-competition testing, they will be asked to provide up-to-date athlete whereabouts filings to ensure they can be tested anytime and anywhere at no advance notice. Athletes who have already been notified and inducted onto UK Anti-Doping's online system, ADAMS, (Anti-Doping Administration and Management System), should ensure that their athlete whereabouts filings are up to date at all times. Visit www.myadams.co.uk to view the ADAMS tutorial.

THERAPEUTIC USE EXEMPTION (TUE)

Athletes who need a prescribed medication or a medical treatment to treat an ongoing or existing medical condition should check whether they contain substances that are prohibited before using them. If there is no alternative treatment available, athletes may need to apply for a TUE.

URINE AND BLOOD TESTING AND ATHLETE RIGHTS

Athletes subject to the anti-doping rules of their sport are eligible for testing at any time. Rigorous procedures surround the testing process; these are strictly followed to ensure the rights of the athlete are protected. Testing involves an athlete giving a urine or blood sample to a highly trained and accredited doping control officer. That sample is then sent to an accredited WADA laboratory for analysis.

Please see full details below:

Anti-Doping Services
Drug information line: +44 (0) 800 528 0004
Drug information email: athlete@ukad.org.uk
Confidential fax: +44 (0) 800 298 3362
Therapeutic use exemption email: tue@ukad.org.uk

Whereabouts Services
Whereabouts System: www.myadams.co.uk
Whereabouts phone line: 008000 943 7378 (not available from USA and Australia)
Whereabouts SMS: +44 (0) 7786 202 407
Whereabouts email: athlete@ukad.org.uk

UK Anti-Doping
Tel: +44 (0) 20 7766 7350
Fax: +44 (0) 20 7766 7351
Email: information@ukad.org.uk
Address:
Oceanic House
1a Cockspur Street
London
SW1Y 5BG

DRUGS

ESSENTIAL CONTACTS

Athletes should not hesitate to ask questions about anti-doping. As well as asking their NGB, coaches and athlete support personnel, athletes can contact the drug information line or UK Anti-Doping directly with their questions. UK Anti-Doping would advise athletes to seek assistance rather than risk an anti-doping rule violation.

THE SAMPLING PROCEDURE

ATHLETE SELECTION

An athlete can be selected for testing anywhere, at any time, and is subject to both random and targeted selection methods.

The role of the doping control officers (DCOs) is to organise and manage the sample collection session, ensuring that all procedures are followed. The role of the chaperone is to notify, accompany and witness the athlete providing a sample.

DCOs and chaperones do not determine the doping control programme, and they do not control who is selected for testing, or how selections are made. Their role is to ensure that sample collection occurs in strict accordance with the relevant procedures, in a fair, equitable manner free from prejudice.

NOTIFICATION

The DCO or chaperone will notify an athlete for sample collection generally in person, or less frequently by telephone, written notice, or by a third party.

At the time of notification, the DCO will present the athlete with a notice and record their details on a doping control notification form. The athlete is required to sign the form and will be provided with a copy for their records.

Once notified of selection for testing, an athlete must remain in direct observation of the DCO or chaperone until the DCO is satisfied that the sample collection procedure is complete. Any attempt to evade notification may result in an anti-doping rule violation.

Third-party notifications

It is recommended that a third party (for example, guardian or coach) is also notified of an athlete's selection for sample collection when an athlete is under the age of 18 or has difficultly communicating verbally in English.

In the case of an athlete with an intellectual disability, it is a requirement that a third party is notified.

If the third party attempts to hinder the notification process or is obstructive, this may be considered to be an anti-doping rule violation, and may result in a sanction for the third party.

REPORTING TO THE DOPING CONTROL STATION

For no-advance-notice testing, including in-competition testing, athletes are required to report to the doping control station immediately unless they request a delay in reporting for valid reasons. Athletes can ask the DCO for information on the sample collection process.

SELECTING A COLLECTION VESSEL

An athlete will be given a choice of individually sealed collection vessels, and will select one. They will then verify that the equipment is intact and has not been tampered with, and will maintain control of the collection vessel at all times.

PROVIDING THE SAMPLE

Urine sample provision

Only a chaperone of the same gender is permitted in the area of privacy when an athlete provides the sample. The chaperone will directly witness the urine sample leaving the body and going into the beaker.

Athletes are required to remove any clothing from the knees to the mid-torso and from the hands to the elbows. This provides the chaperone with a direct view of the urine leaving the body, ensures that it is the athlete's own urine and helps to prevent possible manipulation of the urine sample.

Athletes are responsible for controlling their sample and keeping it in view of the DCO or chaperone until it is sealed in a sample collection kit.

If an athlete provides a sample of less than the required volume, they are required to temporarily seal it and provide further volume.

The first urine sample(s) that an athlete is able to provide post notification must be collected.

Blood sample provision

An athlete will be asked to select blood collection equipment and check that it is intact and has not been tampered with. A blood collection official will collect the sample in the presence of a DCO, chaperone and, if applicable, the athlete representative.

If an athlete has provided a blood sample, it is recommended that they do not do any strenuous exercise using that arm for a minimum of 30 minutes, to minimise bruising at the puncture site.

Athletes with disabilities

If an athlete has a disability, they have the right to request a modification to the process; however, the DCO must approve it. Where required, an athlete will be provided with assistance during the sample collection procedure, and the procedures will be modified where necessary.

If an athlete uses a leg bag, he or she will be required to drain any urine from the leg bag prior to the witnessed sample provision. If possible, athletes are required to use a clean, sterile catheter. If an athlete chooses to use a non-sterile catheter, they do so at their own risk.

Athlete representative

If an athlete is under 18 years of age, they are encouraged to have a representative present while providing a urine sample. The representative will not directly witness the athlete providing the sample unless they are specifically requested to do so.

If an athlete has a disability and requires a representative, they will not directly witness the provision of the sample unless the athlete requires their assistance to provide a sample.

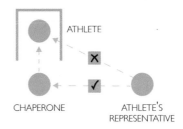

Figure 3.1 Viewpoint of the athlete's representative

QUESTIONS

Level 2

Q.1. Briefly describe the sampling procedure employed by WADA, and other similar bodies around the world, in order to detect doping offences.

Q.2. Anabolic steroids are commonly used to improve performance in sport. Explain what anabolic steroids are, how they work and the side effects associated with their use.

Q.3. Athletes who need to take medication may obtain a therapeutic use exemption (TUE). Explain what is meant by a TUE and what an athlete must do in order to obtain one.

Q.4. WADA employs the principles of strict liability in relation to doping offences. Explain what is meant by strict liability.

Q.5. It is WADA policy to work in co-operation with the law enforcement agencies of all national governments. List the likely consequences of this decision upon the investigative methods employed to detect doping offences.

Q.6. The WADA *Prohibited List* itemises 14 classifications of banned substances and banned methods. List six of these in simple layman's terms that you could use to explain to an athlete.

Level 3

Q.1. An athlete who trains at your gym has been selected to participate in a sporting event at which he will be subject to doping control in accordance with the sampling procedures employed by WADA. Advise the athlete on the ways in which he or she might prepare for the sampling procedure.

Q.2. Diuretics are contained on the *Prohibited List*. What is a diuretic and why is it included on the list?

Q.3. Where can an athlete go if he or she requires additional information about a drug that has been prescribed?

Q.4. In 2002, Alain Baxter made Olympic history by becoming the first Briton to win a medal at the Winter Olympics, when he won a bronze in the alpine skiing event at Salt Lake City. Explain the circumstances that led to that medal being taken away from him.

Q.5. The *Prohibited List* itemises 14 classifications of banned substances and banned methods. List eight of these in simple layman's terms that you could use to explain to an athlete and explain the reasons that they have been included on the list.

Q.6. The *Prohibited List* is defined in a way that allows it to be flexible to changes in knowledge. Explain how this has been achieved.

Level 4

Q.1. One of the 'hot topics' in doping at present relates to growth hormone. Explain what growth hormone is and why it is a particularly contentious subject.

Q.2. An athlete who has taken a banned substance on the *Prohibited List* and who is then required to take a test may employ the technique known as a 'diuretic flush'. What is this?

Q.3. Item M1 on the *Prohibited List* is enhancement of oxygen transfer. Explain why this was added to the list and the issues surrounding the techniques.

Q.4. It has been said that some professional athletes may take 'social drugs'. What are social drugs and what are the issues that are raised when athletes subject to drug testing take social drugs?

Q.5. The *Prohibited List* itemises 14 classifications of banned substances and banned methods. List 10 of these in simple layman's terms that you could use to explain to an athlete. Set out the reasons why athletes may want to use these drugs and methods, and the side effects that their use may have on the athlete.

Q.6. An athlete who trains at your gym has been selected to participate in a sporting event at which he or she will be subject to doping control in accordance with the sampling procedures employed by WADA. Set out the procedures that will be followed, the ways in which he or she may prepare for the testing and the responsibilities that this places on him or her and the ways in which he or she should behave.

EXERCISES

4

IMPORTANT NOTICE

Olympic weightlifting exercises are usually performed without a spotter, as the weights may safely be allowed to fall to the ground.

Nearly all other free weight exercises require one or two spotters in order to prevent the risk of serious injury. Spotting is an important skill and is covered in detail in chapter 2.

A great deal of effort has been taken to produce the following section. Its aim to the focus attention on the detail that goes into techniques each, to permit the heaviest weights to be lifted safely. All spotters and machinery that detracted from the clarity of the photos in this chapter have been digitally removed.

I would like the readers to be aware that a sufficient number of trained spotters were available when these photographs were taken, as is the case in all sessions that I coach, and that I do not condone training without the protection that spotters afford.

The exercises

Note: Standard weights for male and female are indicated by the following M = Male, F = Female.

EXERCISES

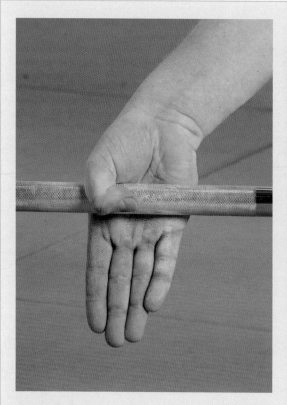
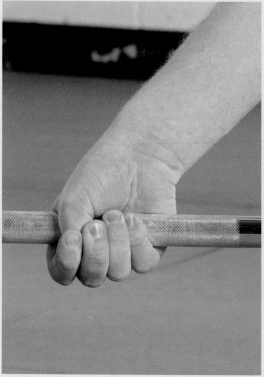

Hook grip

When starting to lift weights, many athletes use the simple, obvious grip and this will suffice while lifting light weights. However, the best weightlifting bars are made of 90-ton tensile steel and may be used to lift extremely heavy weights, sometimes well in excess of half a ton.

These weights cause the bar to bend, so that in the dead lift, athletes lifting the heaviest weights may raise the bar several centimetres before the weights leave the floor. If a bar that has bent in this way rotates, then it will break the athlete's grip on the bar, unless the athlete has employed a hook grip, which is exceptionally strong. This grip is achieved by taking a simple grip and then placing the thumb along the line of the bar and gripping the bar and the thumb with the four fingers.

A hook grip may be uncomfortable for a few days when first used, but quickly becomes painless and familiar. A hook grip may be used in any exercise.

EXERCISE 1: GET SET POSITION

PURPOSE

This is the starting position for all lifts in which the weight is lifted from the floor; it teaches an athlete the important skill of back management, which will protect the back from injury throughout life, whatever exercise is performed.

KEY POSITIONS AND ACTIONS

1   Step up to the bar and stand erect with feet hip-width apart, toes turned slightly out to the side. This should be a very stable position. As you look down, the bar should appear to cut the toes off the feet. This fixes the distance between the lifter and the bar.

2   Push the chest out and the shoulders back in order to straighten and strengthen the back. Tilt forward 45 degrees from the hips and bend the knees so as to lower the upper body towards the bar and keep the back straight and tight. Let the arms hang naturally until the hands touch the bar. Do not reach to take hold of the bar, as this will cause the shoulders to round and the back to bend.

3   Grip the bar with a palms downward grip, slightly wider than shoulder-width apart, and in the hook style (*see* opposite). Fix the eyes on a point on the floor 2m in front of the bar, so as to fix the position of the head, eliminate distractions and aid concentration.

4   When ready to lift, take a sharp intake of breath, hold it and start the lift by raising the head.

MUSCLES USED

None, this is a stationary position. Many muscles are in static contraction to hold the get set position.

BREATHING

Normal breathing.

EXERCISE 2: POWER CLEAN

	M	F	M	F	M	F	M	F
Bodyweight kg	60	50	77	60	94	70	108	75
Novice	62	26	77	40	83	47	89	50
Club	73	39	88	49	98	54	105	57
Champion	92	44	111	60	122	68	131	72

PURPOSE

This is the simplest, most basic form of the clean, the first part of the clean and jerk, which is the second of the two Olympic lifts. It is an all-round power-building exercise and is used in a number of exercises in which the bar is raised from the floor to the chest.

KEY POSITIONS AND ACTIONS

1 Get set position: follow the instructions given on page 59 to get into the starting position.

2 Bar at just below knee height: start to straighten the legs so as to bring the bar up to just below knee height. At the same time, draw the bar just a little closer towards you so as to keep yourself in balance and stop yourself from falling forwards.

3 Maximum upward extension: completely straighten the legs and vigorously extend the hips so as to raise the bar as high as your strength will allow without bending the elbows, which you should not do. This is the position that determines whether you succeed or fail the lift. If you can pull the bar close to the height of the chest then you should be able to clean the weight and only poor technique should stop you.

4 Receiving position: having raised the bar as high as you can in (3), quickly pull yourself down underneath the bar in order to secure the bar on your chest. In the power clean this means that you simply bend your legs slightly in order to absorb the force of the weight as it lands on you, which protects your knees and back from injury.

5 Finishing position: you then vigorously straighten your legs so that you stand erect with the bar fixed onto the top of your chest by your elbows held high.

MUSCLES USED

This is as close as it is possible to get to using all the muscles in the body in one exercise. The exercise particularly focuses on the muscles on the front of the upper leg, the back, and the hip extensors (erector spinae and trapezius, rectus femoris, vastus [lateralis, intermedius and medialis], gluteus maximus and medius, fascia lata, biceps femoris). When doing this, you use your strongest muscles, those at the front of the upper legs and the lower back, twice. These muscles raised the bar off the ground by straightening between (1) (2), then bending between (3) and (4) so that they could straighten again between (4) and (5).

BREATHING

Breathe in as you raise the bar to the chest and breathe out as you settle the bar on the chest.

EXERCISE 3: SQUAT CLEAN

	M	F	M	F	M	F	M	F
Bodyweight kg	60	50	77	60	94	70	108	75
Novice	69	31	85	45	92	52	99	55
Club	81	39	98	53	109	60	117	64
Champion	102	48	123	66	136	75	146	80

PURPOSE

This is the most efficient way to clean a bar to the chest, which is the first part of the clean and jerk, the second of the two Olympic lifts. It is an all-round power-building exercise. The squat clean is used in a number of exercises in which the bar is raised from the floor to the chest.

KEY POSITIONS AND ACTIONS

1   Get set position: follow the instructions given on page 59 to get into the starting position.

2 Bar at just below knee height: start to straighten the legs so as to bring the bar up to just below knee height. At the same time, draw the bar just a little closer towards you so as to keep yourself in balance.

3 Maximum upward extension: completely straighten the legs and vigorously extend your hips so as to raise the bar as high as your strength will allow you without bending your elbows, which you should not do. This is the position that determines whether you succeed or fail the lift. If you can touch your belt with the bar then you should be able to squat clean the weight and only poor technique should stop you.

4 Receiving position: having raised the bar as high as you can in (3), quickly pull yourself down as far as you can underneath the bar in order to secure the bar onto your chest. Jumping the feet slightly forwards and outwards will assist in a strong receiving position. In the squat clean, you bend your legs into a full squat so as to be able to lift the maximum weight.

5 Finishing position: vigorously straighten your legs so that you stand erect with the bar fixed onto the top of your chest by your elbows held high.

MUSCLES USED

This is as close as it is possible to get to using all the muscles in the body in one exercise. The exercise particularly focuses on the muscles on the front of the upper leg, the back and the hip extensors (erector spinae and trapezius, rectus femoris, vastus [lateralis, intermedius and medialis], gluteus maximus and medius, fascia lata, biceps femoris). In this way you have been able to use your strongest muscles, those in the front of your upper legs and the lower back, twice. These muscles raised the bar off the ground by straightening between (1) and (2), then bending between (3) and (4) so that they could straighten again between (4) and (5). How efficient is *that*?

BREATHING

Breathe in as you raise the bar to the chest and breathe out as you settle the bar on the chest.

EXERCISE 4: POWER SNATCH

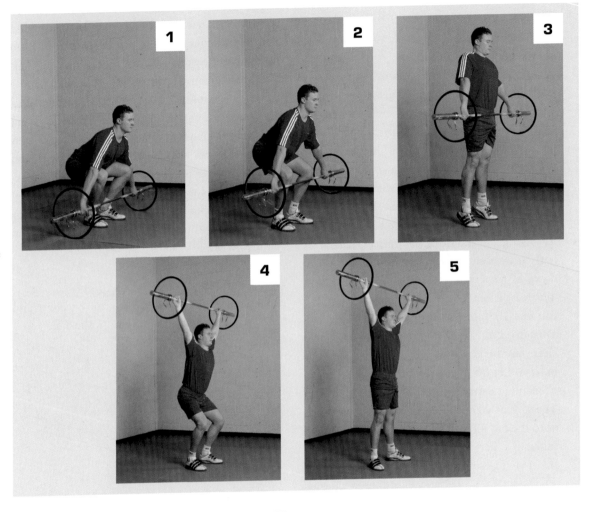

	M	F	M	F	M	F	M	F
Bodyweight kg	**60**	**50**	**77**	**60**	**94**	**70**	**108**	**75**
Novice	47	20	57	30	62	35	67	37
Club	55	26	67	36	74	41	79	44
Champion	69	35	83	45	92	51	99	54

PURPOSE

This is the simplest, most basic form of the snatch, which is the first of the Olympic lifts, in which the weight is taken from the floor to arm's length overhead in one movement. It is an all-round power-building exercise.

KEY POSITIONS AND ACTIONS

1 Get set position: follow the instructions given on page 59 to get into the starting position. As your grip is considerably wider than it was in the clean, you will find that

your head and shoulders are lower than they were previously.

2   Bar at just below knee height: start to straighten the legs so as to bring the bar up to just below knee height. At the same time, draw the bar just a little closer towards you so as to keep yourself in balance.

3   Maximum upward extension: completely straighten the legs and extend your hips so as to raise the bar as high as your strength will allow. This is the position that determines whether you succeed or fail the lift. Now lift the shoulders as high as possible and simultaneously pull strongly with the arms, elbows out to the sides, to bring the bar to the height of your chest. You should be able to snatch the weight having achieved this position.

4   Receiving position: having raised the bar as high as you can in (3), now quickly pull yourself down underneath the bar in order to secure the bar overhead. In the power snatch this means that you simply bend your legs slightly in order to absorb the force of the weight as it lands on you, which protects your knees and back from injury.

5   Finishing position: vigorously straighten your legs so that you stand erect with the bar fixed at arm's length overhead. The bar should be held at arm's length vertically above shoulders with arms fully extended.

MUSCLES USED

This is as close as it is possible to get to using all the muscles in the body in one exercise. The exercise particularly focuses on the muscles on the front of the upper leg, the back and the hip extensors (erector spinae and trapezius, rectus femoris, vastus [lateralis, intermedius and medialis], gluteus maximus and medius, fascia lata, biceps femoris). In this way you have been able to use your strongest muscles, those in the front of your upper legs and the lower back, twice. These muscles raised the bar off the ground by straightening between (1) and (2), then bending between (3) and (4) so that they could straighten again between (4) and (5).

BREATHING

Breathe in as you raise the bar to arm's length overhead and breathe out as you fix the bar overhead.

Measuring the grip

There are two ways of measuring the grip for the snatch: the first method is to measure from the end of one hand when it is clenched into a fist, across the back to the other shoulder; the other method is to measure from elbow to elbow across the shoulders. The distance should be the same whichever method is used; this is then marked across the middle of the bar so as to provide a balanced grip for the lifter.

EXERCISE 5: SQUAT SNATCH

	M	F	M	F	M	F	M	F
Bodyweight kg	**60**	**50**	**77**	**60**	**94**	**70**	**108**	**75**
Novice	52	24	63	34	69	39	74	41
Club	61	30	74	40	82	45	88	48
Champion	77	36	92	50	102	57	110	60

PURPOSE

This is the most efficient form of the snatch, which is the first of the Olympic lifts, in which the weight is taken from the floor to arm's length overhead in one movement.

KEY POSITIONS AND ACTIONS

1   Get set position: follow the instructions given on page 59 to get into the starting position. As your grip is considerably wider that it was in the clean, you will find that your head and shoulders are lower than they were previously.

2 Bar at just below knee height: start to straighten the legs so as to bring the bar up to just below knee height. At the same time, draw the bar just a little closer towards you so as to keep yourself in balance.

3 Maximum upward extension: completely straighten the legs and extend your hips so as to raise the bar as high as your strength will allow without bending your elbows, which you should not do. This is the position that determines whether you succeed or fail the lift. If you can reach belt height with the bar then you should be able to snatch the weight and only poor technique should stop you.

4 Receiving position: having raised the bar as high as you can in (3), you now try to pull yourself down underneath the bar in order to secure the bar overhead. In the squat snatch you bend your legs into a full squat so as to be able to lift the maximum weight.

5 Finishing position: vigorously straighten your legs so that you stand erect with the bar fixed at arm's length overhead. The bar should be held at arm's length vertically above shoulders with arms fully extended.

MUSCLES USED

This is as close as it is possible to get to using all the muscles in the body in one exercise. The exercise particularly focuses on the muscles on the front of the upper leg, the back and the hip extensors (erector spinae and trapezius, rectus femoris, vastus [lateralis, intermedius and medialis]). In this way you have been able to use your strongest muscles, those in the front of your upper legs and the lower back, twice. These muscles raised the bar off the ground by straightening between (1) and (2), then bent between (3) and (4) so that they could straighten again between (4) and (5). How efficient is *that*?

BREATHING

Breathe in as you raise the bar to arm's length overhead and breathe out as you fix the bar overhead.

Measuring the grip

There are two ways of measuring the grip for the snatch: the first method is to measure from the end of one hand when it is clenched into a fist, across the back to the other shoulder; the other method is to measure from elbow to elbow across the shoulders. The distance should be the same whichever method is used; this is then marked across the middle of the bar so as to provide a balanced grip for the lifter.

EXERCISE 6: PRESS

	M	F	M	F	M	F	M	F
Bodyweight kg	60	50	77	60	94	70	108	75
Novice	52	24	64	34	69	39	75	42
Club	61	30	74	40	82	45	89	48
Champion	77	36	92	50	102	57	111	60

PURPOSE

To improve overhead lifting, to strengthen and develop the muscles of the shoulders, upper back and back of the upper arm.

KEY POSITIONS AND ACTIONS

1   Starting position: stand erect with feet shoulder-width apart. Hold the bar on the top of the chest with the elbows held high. It is possible to achieve this position in two ways: either by cleaning the bar to the chest or by taking the bar out of a rack and stepping forward or backward in order to find space to move. Fix the eyes on a spot straight in front of you at eye level, so as to stop the head bobbing up and down and therefore prevent unnecessary movement.

2   Movement: vigorously straighten the arms while keeping the rest of the body still. Press the bar out to arm's length.

3   Finishing position: standing erect with feet hip-width apart and the bar locked out at arm's length overhead.

MUSCLES USED

The muscles at the top of the chest, across the shoulders and the back of the upper arm (pectoralis major [clavicular part] deltoideus [anterior and middle parts] trapezius, triceps brachii [long and medial heads] and serratus anterior [medialis]).

BREATHING

Breathe in as you press the bar to arm's length overhead and breathe out as you lower the bar under control back to the chest.

EXERCISE 7: ALTERNATE DUMBBELL PRESS

	M	F	M	F	M	F	M	F
Bodyweight kg	60	50	77	60	94	70	108	75
Novice	23	11	28	15	31	17	34	18
Club	27	13	33	18	37	20	40	21
Champion	34	16	42	22	46	25	49	27

PURPOSE

To improve overhead lifting, to strengthen and develop the muscles of the shoulders, upper back and the back of the upper arms, and to eliminate imbalances in the strength of the arms.

KEY POSITIONS AND ACTIONS

1. Starting position: the dumbbells are cleaned to the shoulders and you assume the position shown. The feet are shoulder-width apart and the body is upright with the dumbbells close to the shoulders and the forearms vertical.
2. Movement: from the starting position, extend one arm vigorously, driving the dumbbell upwards from its position by the shoulder to arm's length overhead as shown, while the other arm remains on the shoulder.
3. After two seconds, the dumbbell is lowered under control back to the shoulder. Repeat the exercise using the other arm. Finishing position: the feet are shoulder-width apart and the body is upright with the dumbbells close to the shoulders and the forearms vertical.

MUSCLES USED

The muscles at the top of the chest, across the shoulders, upper back and the back of the upper arm (pectoralis major [clavicular part], deltoideus [anterior and middle parts], trapezius triceps brachii [long and medial heads] and serratus anterior).

BREATHING

Breathe in on the effort of driving the weight from the shoulder and breathe out as it is returned to the starting position.

EXERCISE 8: PRESS BEHIND NECK

	M	F	M	F	M	F	M	F
Bodyweight kg	60	50	77	60	94	70	108	75
Novice	46	22	56	30	62	34	67	36
Club	54	25	66	35	73	40	79	43
Champion	68	30	83	44	92	51	98	54

PURPOSE

To improve the overhead lifts and to strengthen and develop the muscles of the shoulder, upper back and the back of the upper arm.

KEY POSITIONS AND ACTIONS

1 Starting position: stand erect with feet shoulder-width apart. Hold the bar on the top of the back with a palms-downward grip on the bar. It is possible to achieve this position in two ways: either by cleaning the bar to the chest, pressing it out to arm's length and then lowering it onto the shoulders; or by taking the bar out of a rack and stepping forward or backward to find space to move.

2 Movement: vigorously straighten the arms while keeping the rest of the body still. Press the bar out to arm's length. Fix the eyes on a spot straight in front of you at eye level, so as to stop the head bobbing up and down and therefore stop unnecessary movement.

3 Finishing position: Standing erect with feet shoulder-width apart and the bar locked out at arm's length overhead.

MUSCLES USED

The shoulders, upper back and the back of the upper arm (deltoids [anterior, posterior and middle], trapezius, triceps brachii [lateral, medial and long heads]).

BREATHING

Breathe in as you press the bar vigorously to arm's length overhead and breathe out as you lower the bar under control back to the shoulders.

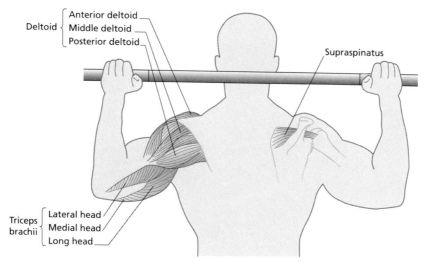

Figure 4.1 Muscles used in the press behind neck

EXERCISE: 9 PUSH PRESS

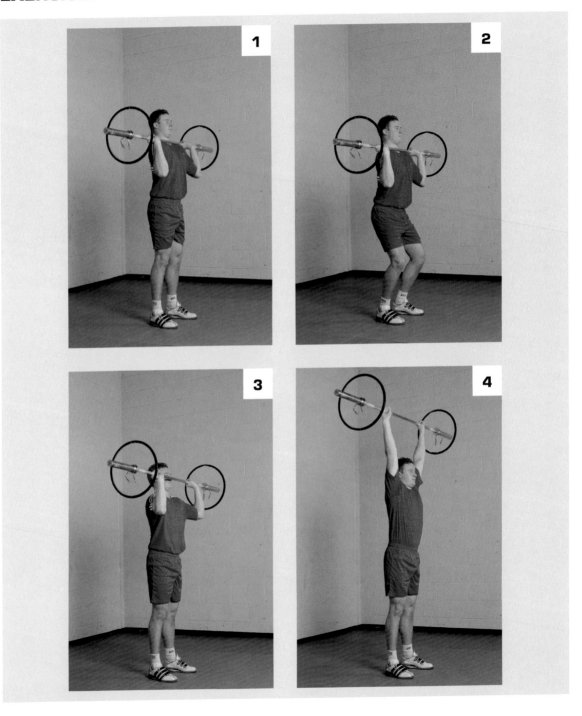

	M	F	M	F	M	F	M	F
Bodyweight kg	60	50	77	60	94	70	108	75
Novice	55	26	68	36	73	41	79	44
Club	65	30	78	42	87	48	94	51
Champion	82	39	98	53	109	60	117	64

PURPOSE

This is a power assistance exercise designed to improve the strength aspects of the jerk, but without the complication of balance and technique.

KEY POSITIONS AND ACTIONS

1   Starting position: stand erect with feet hip-width apart. Hold the bar on the chest with a palms-downward grip on the bar. It is possible to achieve this position in two ways: either by cleaning the bar to the chest or by taking the bar out of a rack and stepping forward or backward to find space to move.

2   The dip: bend the knees so as to lower the body about 5 to 7cm. Fix the eyes on a spot straight in front of you at eye level. Dip only as low as the ankle flexibility will permit while maintaining the feet flat on the floor and keeping the trunk upright.

3   The top of the drive: vigorously straighten the legs and arms so as to drive the bar out to arm's length overhead.

4   The finishing position: stand erect with the bar held at arm's length overhead.

MUSCLES USED

The muscles of the front of the thigh, hips, upper back and the back of the upper arms (rectus femoris, vastus [lateralis, intermedius and medialis] gluteus maximus and medius, fascia lata, biceps temoris, trapezius and triceps brachii).

BREATHING

Breathe in as you are about to drive the bar overhead. Hold your breath as you press the bar out to arm's length and breathe out as you fix the bar overhead.

EXERCISE 10: POWER JERK

	M	F	M	F	M	F	M	F
Bodyweight kg	60	50	77	60	94	70	108	75
Novice	62	32	77	42	83	47	89	50
Club	73	33	88	47	98	54	105	57
Champion	92	44	111	60	122	68	131	72

PURPOSE

This is a power assistance exercise designed to improve the strength aspects of the jerk, but with only a few of the technical and balance problems.

KEY POSITIONS AND ACTIONS

1 Starting position: stand erect with feet hip-width apart. Hold the bar on the chest with a palms-downward grip on the bar. It is possible to achieve this position in two ways: either by cleaning the bar to the chest or by taking the bar out of a rack and stepping forward or backward to find room to move.

2 The dip: bend the knees so as to lower the chest about 5 to 7cms. Keep the elbows high. Fix the eyes on a spot straight in front of you at eye level. Dip only as low as the ankle flexibility will permit while maintaining the feet flat on the floor and keeping the trunk upright.

3 The top of the drive: the power of the legs diminishes as the bar reaches roughly the height of the nose, but the arms then continue the momentum to drive the bar out to arm's length.

4 Receiving position: bend the knees to lower your body so as to be able to lock out the arms under the bar.

5 The finishing position: vigorously straighten the legs so as to stand up and hold the bar at arm's length overhead.

MUSCLES USED

The muscles of the front of the thigh, hips, upper back and the back of the upper arms (rectus femoris, vastus [lateralis, intermedius and medialis], gluteus maximus and medius, fascia lata, biceps femoris, trapezius, triceps brachii).

BREATHING

Breathe in as you are about to drive the bar overhead. Hold your breath as you drive the bar out to arm's length and breathe out as you straighten your legs to finish the lift.

EXERCISE 11: JERK

	M	F	M	F	M	F	M	F
Bodyweight kg	60	50	77	60	94	70	108	75
Novice	69	31	85	45	92	52	99	55
Club	81	39	98	53	109	60	117	64
Champion	102	48	123	66	136	75	146	80

PURPOSE

This is the second part of the clean and jerk, the second of the two Olympic lifts. It is the most efficient way to lift heavy weights overhead.

KEY POSITIONS AND ACTIONS

1 Starting position: stand erect with feet hip-width apart. Hold the bar on the chest with a palms-downward grip on the bar. It is possible to achieve this position in two ways: either by cleaning the bar to the chest or by taking the bar out of a rack and stepping forward or backward to find room to move.

2 The dip: bend the knees so as to lower the chest about 5 to 7cm. Fix the eyes on a spot straight in front of you at eye level. Dip only as low as the ankle flexibility will permit while maintaining the feet flat on the floor and keeping the trunk upright.

3 The top of the drive: the power of the legs diminishes as the bar reaches roughly the height of the nose, but the arms then continue the momentum to drive the bar out to arm's length.

4 Receiving position: split your feet forwards and backwards in order to lower the body and be able to lock out the arms under the bar. While the feet are hip-width apart, the front foot moves straight forward and the back foot moves straight back, so that the hip-width distance between them is maintained. This prevents the lifter 'standing on a tightrope' where the feet are in line and the lifter is unstable and can easily topple over. It is a matter of choice for the lifter which foot goes forward and which goes back.

5 The finishing position: vigorously straighten both legs and step the front foot back to the middle and the back foot forward to the middle, so that the two feet are side by side. Then stand erect holding the bar at arm's length overhead. Any other method is less efficient. If the back foot steps forward, for example, the lifter could be left struggling with a very heavy weight overhead and would have to walk backwards to an area that he or she cannot see, which is undesirable. If, as a result of stepping the front foot backwards, the lifter feels that balance has been lost, the best thing to do is step forwards again in order to secure the bar overhead and recover. In the heat of competition, when a lifter is under great stress, he or she may use other methods to control the weight and keep it overhead.

MUSCLES USED

The muscles of the front of the thigh, hips, upper back and the back of the upper arms (rectus femoris, vastus [lateralis, intermedius and medialis], gluteus maximus and medius, fascia lata, biceps termoris, trapezius, triceps brachii).

BREATHING

Breathe in as you are about to drive the bar overhead. Hold your breath as you drive the bar out to arm's length and breathe out as you finish the lift.

EXERCISE 12: CLEAN PULL

	M	F	M	F	M	F	M	F
Bodyweight kg	60	50	77	60	94	70	108	75
Novice	83	38	102	54	110	62	119	66
Club	97	45	118	63	131	72	140	77
Champion	122	57	148	79	163	90	175	96

PURPOSE

This is a power assistance exercise for the clean.

KEY POSITIONS AND ACTIONS

1　Starting position: follow the instructions given on page 59 to get into the starting position.

2　Movement: strongly drive with the legs and hips to lift from the floor and bring the bar up to just below knee height. At the same time draw the bar just a little closer towards you so as to keep yourself in balance and stop you from falling forwards.

3　Finishing position: completely straighten the legs and vigorously extend your hips so as to raise the bar as high as your strength will allow. This is the position that determines whether you succeed or fail in the clean. If you can get close to the height of your chest with the bar then you should be able to clean the weight and only poor technique should stop you. Some coaches recommend resting a training bar on two squat stands perpendicular to the lifting bar and to one side. In this way the lifter can rattle the training bar every time that he lifts the bar. This is a confirmation that he has lifted the bar as he is supposed to, and can be a target for a tired lifter struggling to lift heavy weights at the end of a training session.

MUSCLES USED

This is as close as it is possible to get to using all the muscles in the body in one exercise. The exercise particularly focuses on the muscles on the front of the upper leg and the hip extensors, lower and upper back, (rectus femoris, vastus [lateralis, intermedius and medialis], erector spinae, trapezius, gluteus maximus and medius, fascia lata, biceps femoris).

BREATHING

Breathe in as you raise the bar as high as you can (which is usually to the top of your hips) and breathe out as you lower the bar under control to the floor.

EXERCISE 13: SNATCH PULL

	M	F	M	F	M	F	M	F
Bodyweight kg	60	50	77	60	94	70	108	75
Novice	62	26	76	40	83	47	89	50
Club	73	37	89	49	98	55	106	58
Champion	92	44	110	60	122	68	132	72

PURPOSE

This is a power assistance exercise for the snatch.

KEY POSITIONS AND ACTIONS

1 Starting position: follow the instructions on page 59 to get into the starting position. As your grip is considerably wider than it was in the clean, you will find that your head and shoulders are lower than they were previously.

2 Movement: strongly drive with the legs and hips to lift from the floor and bring the bar up to just below knee height. At the same time draw the bar just a little closer towards you so as to keep yourself in balance.

3 Finishing position: completely straighten the legs and extend your hips so as to raise the bar as high as your strength will allow you without bending your elbows, which you should not do. This is the position that determines whether you succeed or fail the lift. If you can get close to the height of your chest with the bar then you should be able to snatch the weight and only poor technique should stop you. Some coaches recommend resting a training bar on two squat stands perpendicular to the lifting bar and to one side. In this way the lifter can rattle the training bar every time that he lifts the bar. This is a confirmation that he has lifted the bar as he is supposed to, and can be a target for a tired lifter struggling to lift heavy weights at the end of a training session.

Measuring the grip

There are two ways of measuring the grip for the snatch: the first method is to measure from the end of one hand when it is clenched into a fist, across the back to the other shoulder; the other method is to measure from elbow to elbow across the shoulders. The distance should be the same whichever method is used; this is then marked across the middle of the bar so as to provide a balanced grip for the lifter.

MUSCLES USED

This is as close as it is possible to get to use all the muscles in the body in one exercise. The exercise particularly focuses on the muscles on the front of the upper leg and the hip extensors, lower and upper back (rectus femoris, vastus [lateralis, intermedius and medialis], erector spinae, trapezius, gluteus maximus and medius, fascia lata, biceps femoris).

BREATHING

Breathe in as you raise the bar as high as you can (which is usually to the top of your hips) and breathe out as you lower the bar under control to the floor.

EXERCISE 14: PULL FROM HANG (OR BLOCKS)

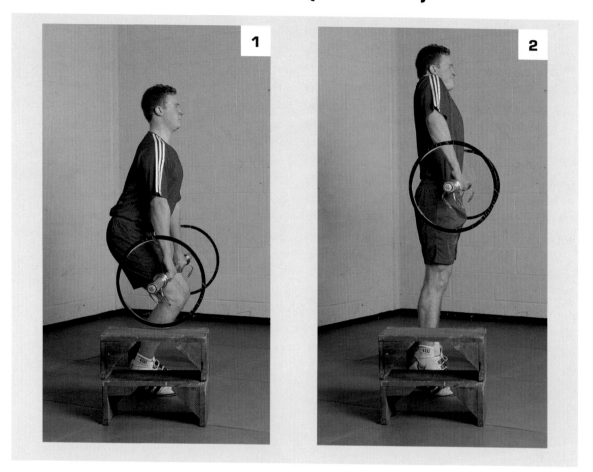

	M	F	M	F	M	F	M	F
Bodyweight kg	60	50	77	60	94	70	108	75
Novice	76	33	94	49	101	57	109	61
Club	89	42	108	58	120	66	129	70
Champion	112	53	135	73	150	83	161	88

PURPOSE

This is a power assistance exercise for the clean. By removing the easier first pull it compels additional effort to achieve the limiting, second (higher) pull.

KEY POSITIONS AND ACTIONS

1   Starting position: the weight is placed on blocks so that the height of the bar is just below the lifter's knees. Follow the instructions given to get into the starting position and powerfully straighten the legs and extend the hips so as to stand erect with the bar reaching the level of the naval. Then lower the bar to the blocks.

2   Movement: completely straighten the legs and vigorously extend your hips so as to raise the bar as high as your strength will allow without bending your elbows, which you should not do. This is the position that determines whether you succeed or fail the lift. If you can get close to the height of your belt with the bar then you should be able to clean the weight and only poor technique should stop you.

3   Finishing position: try to hold the bar at the top before lowering it back down onto the blocks or to just below the height of the knees and repeat the exercise. The blocks can be adjusted in height so that the lift can start both above and below knee height to strengthen different areas of the pull.

MUSCLES USED

This is as close as it is possible to get to using all the muscles in the body in one exercise. The exercise particularly focuses on the muscles on the front of the upper leg and the hip extensors, lower and upper back (rectus femoris, vastus [lateralis, intermedius and medialis], erector spinae and trapezius, gluteus maximus and medius, fascia lata, biceps femoris).

BREATHING

Breathe in as you raise the bar as high as you can (which is usually to the top of your hips) and breathe out as you lower the bar under control to the floor.

EXERCISE 15: DEAD LIFT

	M	F	M	F	M	F	M	F
Bodyweight kg	60	50	77	60	94	70	108	75
Novice	129	63	155	84	172	95	185	101
Club	153	71	184	99	204	113	220	120
Champion	191	90	230	124	255	141	275	150

PURPOSE

An all-round power exercise. Due to the very heavy weights which can be used, the movement tends to be slow, although the lifter is exerting maximum strength throughout.

KEY POSITIONS AND ACTIONS

1   Starting position: follow the instructions previously given to get into the starting position. Use a reverse grip, with one hand facing forward and one hand facing backwards, in order to control the rotation of the bar. It will also be essential to use a hook grip.

2   Movement: strongly drive with the legs and hips so as to bring the bar up to just below knee height. At the same time draw the bar just a little closer towards you so as to keep yourself in balance and stop you from falling forwards.

3   Finishing position: completely straighten the legs and vigorously extend your hips so as to raise the bar to the top of your thighs as you stand erect. Then brace your shoulders back. The bar will rest on the front of the thighs at the end of the movement.

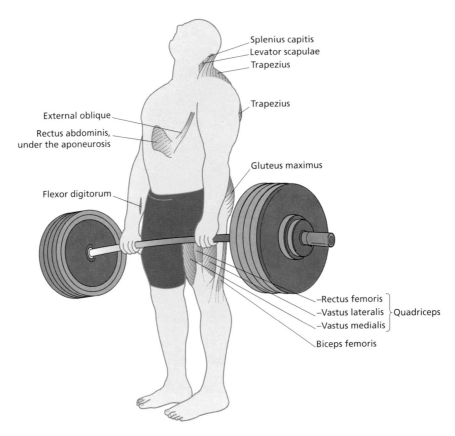

Figure 4.2 Muscles used in dead lift

MUSCLES USED

The muscles of the thighs, hips and back (rectus femoris, vastus [lateralis and medialis], biceps femoris, gluteus maximus, gluteus medius, erector spinae, splenius capitis, levator scapulae, trapezius, levator scapulae, obliquus externus, rectus abdominus and flexor digitorum).

BREATHING

Breathe in as you vigorously straighten up and raise the bar to the thighs and breathe out as you lower it under control back to the floor.

EXERCISE 16: ROMANIAN DEAD LIFT

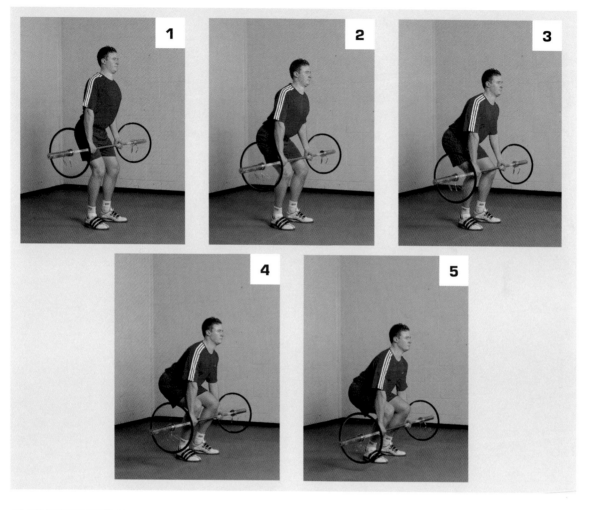

	M	F	M	F	M	F	M	F
Bodyweight kg	60	50	77	60	94	70	108	75
Novice	116	53	140	75	155	86	167	91
Club	138	66	166	90	184	102	198	108
Champion	172	92	207	112	230	127	248	135

PURPOSE

An all-round power exercise.

KEY POSITIONS AND ACTIONS

1   Starting position: follow the instructions given on page 59 to get into the starting position. Use a reverse grip as shown, with one hand facing forward and one hand facing backwards, in order to control the rotation of the bar. It will also be essential to use a hook grip.

2   Movement: completely straighten the legs and vigorously extend your hips so as to raise the bar as high as your strength will allow you without bending your elbows, which you should not do. From this position the bar is now lowered until the weights are 5cm from the floor. During this movement the hips are pushed backwards and a strong stretch should be felt on the hamstrings and hips. The back should be held flat at a 45-degree angle with the head up and arms straight. The body should now be raised, keeping the stretch on the hamstrings and hips until the bar is brought into the hip joint area.

3   Finishing position: the body does not come up to the fully erect position, thus keeping constant tension on the hamstrings, hips and back.

MUSCLES USED

The muscles of the thighs, hips and back (rectus femoris, vastus [lateralis and medialis], biceps femoris, gluteus maximus and medius, trapezius, erector spinae, levator scapulae, obliquus externus, rectus abdominus and flexor digitorum).

BREATHING

Breathe in as you raise the bar to the starting position, breathe out as the bar is lowered towards the floor.

EXERCISE 17: UPRIGHT ROWING

	M	F	M	F	M	F	M	F
Bodyweight kg	60	50	77	60	94	70	108	75
Novice	46	22	56	30	62	34	66	36
Club	55	26	66	36	73	41	79	43
Champion	68	32	82	44	81	50	98	53

PURPOSE

To improve pulling power and develop your shoulders and upper back.

KEY POSITIONS AND ROWING

1 Starting position: stand erect with your feet hip-width apart. Then take a palms-downward grip on the bar, approximately shoulder-width apart, and allow the bar to rest on the thighs.

2 Movement: breathe in, raise the bar to the top of the chest while keeping the elbows above the bar.

3 Finishing position: stand erect with the bar at the top of the chest with the elbows held high. Lower the bar to the starting position allowing arms to fully extend.

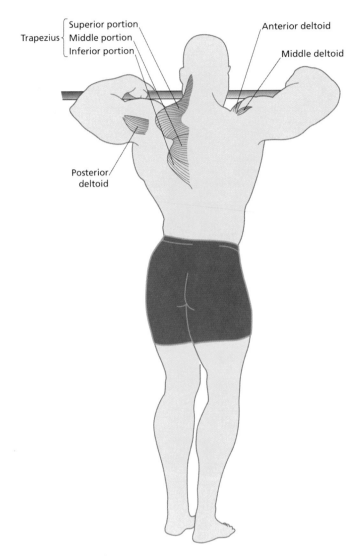

Trapezius {
Superior portion
Middle portion
Inferior portion

Anterior deltoid

Middle deltoid

Posterior/deltoid

Figure 4.3 Muscles used in upright rowing

MUSCLES USED

The muscles at the top of the shoulders, upper back and front of the upper arm (trapezius [superior, middle and inferior] deltoid [posterior, anterior and middle parts] levator scapulae and biceps brachii and brachioradialis).

BREATHING

Breathe in as you raise the bar to the top of the chest and breathe out as you lower it under control back to the thighs.

EXERCISE 18: BENT FORWARD ROWING

	M	F	M	F	M	F	M	F
Bodyweight kg	60	50	77	60	94	70	108	75
Novice	46	11	56	15	62	17	66	18
Club	56	14	66	18	74	20	80	21
Champion	68	16	82	22	82	25	98	27

PURPOSE

To strengthen and develop the muscles of the upper and lower back.

KEY POSITIONS AND ACTIONS

1   Starting positions: get into the get set position and simply stand up so that the bar is resting across the thighs. Then take half a pace out with the left foot, unlock the knees and tilt forward 45 degrees from the hips. In this way, you assume the position shown in figure 4.18 (c) with the bar in front of the knees.

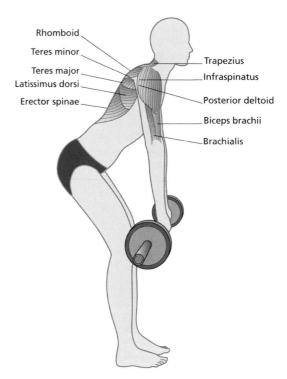

Figure 4.4 Muscles used in bent forward rowing

2 Movement: raise the bar to the top of the chest and keep the elbows higher than the bar.

3 Finishing position: stand in the bent forward position with the bar held at the top of the chest with the elbows higher than the bar. Lower the bar under control until the discs touch the floor with arms fully extended.

MUSCLES USED

The muscles of the upper and lower back and the front of the upper arm (trapezius, rhomboid, infraspinatus, teres minor, teres major, brachialis, bicep brachii, latissimus dorsi, erector spinae, posterior deltoid).

BREATHING

Breathe in as you raise the bar to the top of the chest and breathe out as you lower it under control.

EXERCISE 19: SHRUGS

	M	F	M	F	M	F	M	F
Bodyweight kg	**60**	**50**	**77**	**60**	**94**	**70**	**108**	**75**
Novice	76	33	94	49	101	57	109	61
Club	89	42	108	58	120	66	129	70
Champion	112	53	135	73	150	83	161	88

PURPOSE

To strengthen and develop the muscles of the top of the shoulder and the upper back.

KEY POSITIONS AND ACTIONS

1 Starting position: stand erect with the feet hip-width apart with the bar resting across the thighs. Use a palms-downward grip on the bar, slightly wider than shoulder-width apart.

2 Movement: keeping the arms straight, shrug your shoulders up as high as possible in order to raise the bar. Many lifters use the final repetition of every set in order to exaggerate the movement by rolling the shoulders in a circle, going up, back and down to completely develop the muscles of the shoulder.

3 Finishing position: stand erect with the bar resting across the thighs with the shoulders elevated.

Trapezius, upper portion

MUSCLES USED

The muscles of the top of the shoulder and the upper back (trapezius [superior part] levator scapulae and rhomboids).

BREATHING

Breathe in as you shrug the bar up and breathe out as you relax and lower it under control.

Figure 4.5 Muscles used in shrugs

EXERCISE 20: STRAIGHT LEG DEAD LIFT

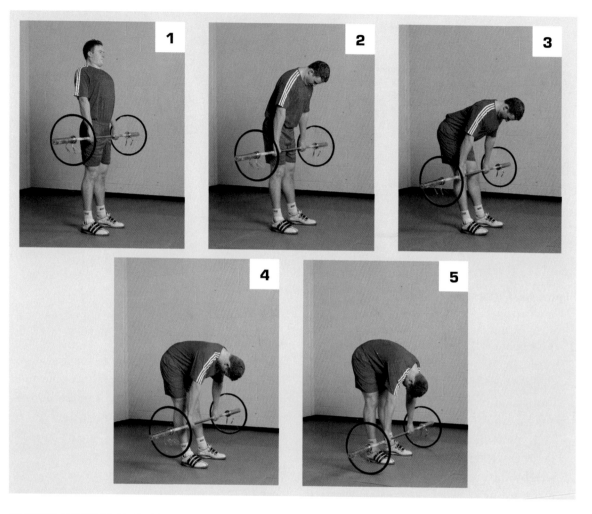

	M	F	M	F	M	F	M	F
Bodyweight kg	60	50	77	60	94	70	108	75
Novice	77	36	93	50	103	57	111	60
Club	92	44	110	60	122	68	132	72
Champion	115	55	138	75	153	85	165	90

Warning: This exercise will make a strong back stronger. It may cause serious injury to an untrained or unfit athlete, who should not undertake the exercise.

PURPOSE

To develop and strengthen the muscles of the hips, lower back and back of the upper legs.

KEY POSITIONS AND ACTIONS

1 Starting position: a very light weight should be used in order to avoid injury when starting this exercise. Stand erect with the bar resting across the thighs.

93

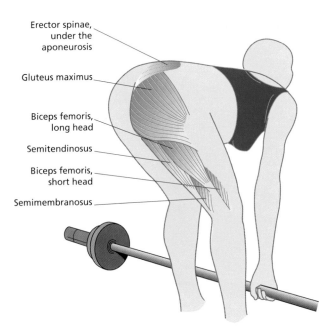

Figure 4.6 Muscles used in the straight leg dead lift

2 Movement: tuck the chin into your chest and gradually flex the trunk forward with legs slightly bent at knees. Your head should go down to or even below your waist by the end and the bar will hang down at the end of your arms and almost reach the floor. The back here is rounded, something that all weightlifters usually strive to avoid. It is permitted here, under careful supervision, in order to specifically strengthen the back and inter-verebral muscles.

3 Finishing position: knees slightly bent and trunk fully flexed forward, head tucked onto chest.

MUSCLES USED

The muscles of the hips, the lower and upper back and the back of the thighs (gluteus maximus and medius, biceps femoris, semitendinosus, semimembranosus, erector spinae and inter-vertebral muscles).

BREATHING

Breathe in as you raise the bar to the thighs and breathe out as you lower it under control back to the floor.

EXERCISE 21: FRONT SQUAT

	M	F	M	F	M	F	M	F
Bodyweight kg	60	50	77	60	94	70	108	75
Novice	78	37	95	51	105	58	113	62
Club	93	42	112	60	124	69	134	73
Champion	116	59	139	77	155	86	167	90

PURPOSE

A very heavy lower-body exercise and a real strength builder. In comparison with the back squat (page 96), the weight is held further forward and over the toes. It is therefore more dynamic and more appropriate to use when attempting to improve performance in the Olympic lifts and when focusing on fast movements.

KEY POSITIONS AND ACTIONS

1   Starting position: stand erect with the bar held on the chest by the arms held high. There are two ways to get the bar into this position: it may be cleaned from the floor or it may be taken from racks. The feet are planted firmly on the floor, shoulder-width apart with the toes turned out to approximately 45 degrees.

2   Movement: bend the knees and lower the body under control until the hips are lower than the knees. The knees use the angle of the feet as tramlines and mirror the same angle. There is a tendency is some lifters to allow the knees to pull closer together, but this must be strongly resisted to avoid twisting movements in the knee. Then vigorously straighten your legs, keeping the knees moving along the same lines as the feet until you have returned to the starting position. This must be a very precise movement because some weightlifters perform as many as 30 squats every day with very heavy

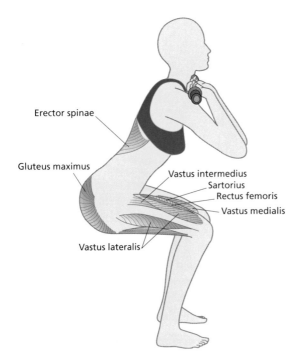

Figure 4.7 Muscles used in front squat

weights and any minor deviation will inevitably lead to chronic injury over the years of training. The movement down should be performed slowly and the movement up is as fast as you can control. The depth of the squat should be a full range movement unless there is a very good reason for not doing so.

3   Finishing position: stand erect with the bar held on the chest by the elbows held high. You may then decide whether to repeat the exercise or return the bar to the rack.

MUSCLES USED
The muscles of the front of the thigh and the hips (rectus femoris, sartorius, erector spinae, vastus [lateralis, intermedius and medialis], gluteus maximus and medius, fascia lata, biceps femoris).

BREATHING
Breathe in as you squat down and breathe out as you vigorously straighten your legs to stand up again. Advanced lifters, with high levels of fitness, will breathe in before they squat down, hold their breath as they squat down and drive up again and then breathe out when they have finished the squat.

Holding the bar
The correct way to hold the bar (a). There is also an alternative way to hold the bar if you lack shoulder flexibility (b), though this technique makes it difficult to dump the bar if you get into difficulties.

EXERCISE 22: BACK SQUAT

	M	F	M	F	M	F	M	F
Bodyweight kg	60	50	77	60	94	70	108	75
Novice		92	44	111	60	123	68	132	72
Club		109	53	131	71	145	80	157	85
Champion		136	62	164	88	182	101	196	107

PURPOSE

This is the greatest lower-body exercise. A real strength builder. Use the high hold (normal) and low hold (competitive power lifters).

KEY POSITIONS AND ACTIONS

1   Starting position: stand erect, holding the bar on the back with your arms. Invariably the bar will be taken from racks, but novices may clean it from the floor, press overhead and lower onto the shoulders in order to get into this position. The feet are planted firmly on the floor, shoulder-width apart with the toes turned out to approximately 45 degrees.

2   Movement: bend your knees and lower the body until the hips are lower than the knees. The knees use the angle of the feet as tramlines and mirror the same angle. There is a tendency is some lifters to allow the knees to pull closer together, but this must be strongly resisted to avoid twisting movements in the knee. The lifter must realise that this lift is not just about using the legs and that it is equally important to keep the back straight and tight and to extend the hips forward at all times. This must be a very precise movement because some weightlifters performs as many as 30 squats every day with very heavy weights and any minor deviation will inevitably lead to chronic injury over the years of training. The

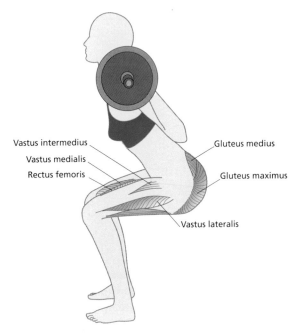

4.8 Muscles used in back squat

Labels: Vastus intermedius, Vastus medialis, Rectus femoris, Gluteus medius, Gluteus maximus, Vastus lateralis

maximus and medius, the biceps femoris and the gastrocnemius and soleus).

BREATHING

Breathe in as you squat down and breathe out as you vigorously straighten your legs to stand up again. Advanced lifters will breathe in before they squat down, hold their breath as they squat down and drive up again and then breathe out when they have finished the squat.

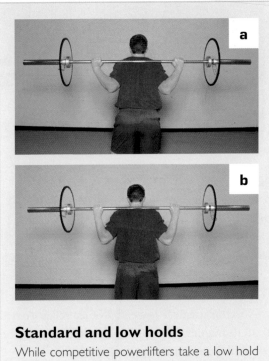

Standard and low holds

While competitive powerlifters take a low hold in order to lift more weight (a) it is safer and more anatomically correct to take a high hold while performing the back squat (b).

movement down should be performed very slowly and the movement up is as fast as you can control. The depth of the squat should be a full range movement unless there is a very good reason for not doing so.

3 Finishing position: vigorously straighten the legs, keeping the knees moving along the same lines of the feet until you have returned to the starting position and are standing erect, with the bar held on the chest by the elbows held high. You may then decide whether to repeat the exercise or return the bar to the rack.

MUSCLES USED

The muscles of the front of the thigh, the hips and the calves (rectus femoris, erector spinae, vastus [lateralis, intermedius and medialis], gluteus

EXERCISE 23: LEG EXTENSION

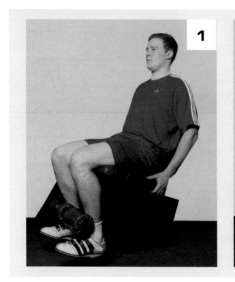 

PURPOSE

To strengthen and tone the muscles at the front of the upper leg.

KEY POSITIONS AND ACTIONS

1   Starting position: adjust the machine so as to suit your size and shape. Take care in sitting in the chair. Push your lower back into the chair and ensure that you can move your knees and ankles in the way that you want to.

2   Movement: this exercise is designed to focus on the muscles at the front of the upper thigh and the best effect is achieved by straightening the legs, then pulling the toes towards the chest and holding this position for a second or two.

3   Finishing position: sitting on the machine with the legs straight and the toes pulled towards the chest. Then relax the ankles and allow the toes to extend, then bend the knees slowly to return the legs to the starting position in order to either repeat the exercise or to finish it.

MUSCLES USED

The muscles of the front of the upper leg (vastus [medialis, lateralis, intermedius], rectus femoris).

BREATHING

Breathe in as you straighten the leg and raise the weight and breathe out as you bend the leg and lower the weight back to the starting position.

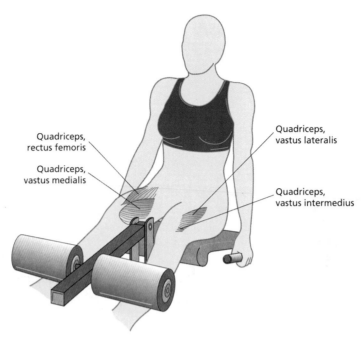

Quadriceps,
rectus femoris

Quadriceps,
vastus medialis

Quadriceps,
vastus lateralis

Quadriceps,
vastus intermedius

Figure 4.9 Muscles used in leg extension

EXERCISE 24: LEG BICEP CURL

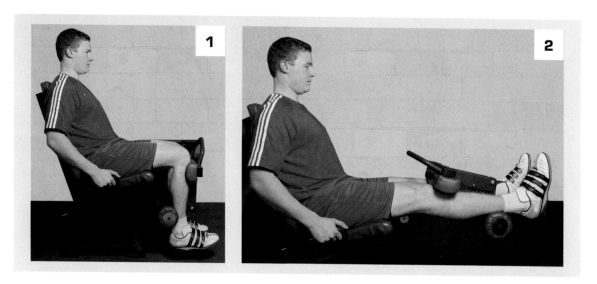

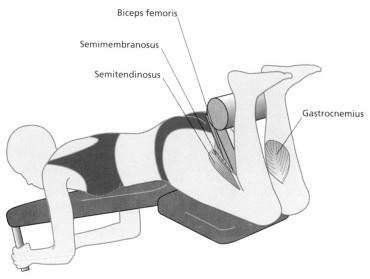

Figure 4.10 Muscles used in leg bicep curl

PURPOSE

To strengthen and tone the muscles of the back of the upper leg and the hips.

KEY POSITIONS AND ACTIONS

1 Starting position: you can perform this exercise either sitting upright (see photographs) or lying on your stomach (see

illustration), depending on the machines available at your gym. If lying prone, ensure that you take care getting into position and that your knees are not resting on the machine, but rather extending just beyond it.

2   Movement: this exercise is designed to focus on the muscles at the back of the upper thigh. Bend the leg as far as you can, point the toes down and hold the position for a second or two. The movement should be slow and sure.

3   Finishing position: relax the ankles and toes before straightening the knees slowly to return the legs to their starting position.

MUSCLES USED
The muscles of the back of the upper leg and the hips (biceps femoris [long and shortheads], semimembranosus, semitendinosus, gastrocnemius).

BREATHING
Breathe in as you bend the leg and raise the weight and breathe out as you straighten the leg and lower the weight under control.

EXERCISE 25: SEATED CALF RAISE

	M	F	M	F	M	F	M	F
Bodyweight kg	60	50	77	60	94	70	108	75
Novice	23	11	28	15	31	17	33	18
Club	28	14	33	18	37	20	40	21
Champion	34	16	41	22	41	25	49	27

Figure 4.11 Muscles used in seated calf raise

PURPOSE

To develop and strengthen the muscles of the lower leg.

KEY POSITIONS AND ACTIONS

1 Starting position: sit erect with both feet on the foot pad and with the barbell resting cross both knees.

2 Movement: flex your ankles so that your toes are higher than your heels. Then extend the ankles so that the toes are lower than the heels. Ensure that you get a full range of movement in each direction.

3 Finishing position: sitting with straight back with the ankles flexed so that the toes are higher than the heels.

MUSCLES USED

The muscles of the lower leg (the gastrocnemius [lateral and medial heads] soleus and plantaris and the tibialis posterior).

BREATHING

Breathe in as you rise up on to your toes and breathe out as you lower your heels back to the ground.

EXERCISE 26: LEG PRESS

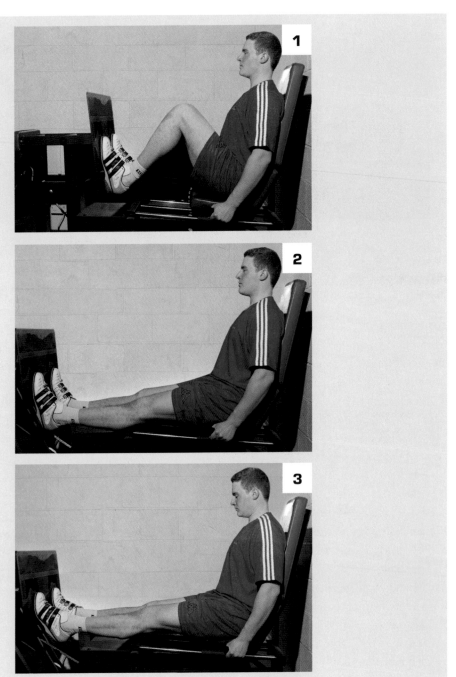

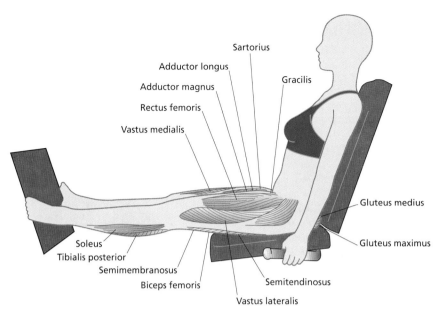

Muscles used in the leg press

Sartorius
Adductor longus
Adductor magnus
Rectus femoris
Vastus medialis
Gracilis
Gluteus medius
Gluteus maximus
Soleus
Tibialis posterior
Semimembranosus
Biceps femoris
Semitendinosus
Vastus lateralis

Figure 4.12 Muscles used in the leg press

PURPOSE

To develop and strengthen the muscles on the front of the upper leg and the hip extensors.

KEY POSITIONS AND ACTIONS

1 Starting position: adjust the machine so as to suit your size and shape. Sit on the chair and place your feet on the force plate in front of you. Take hold of the grips at the side of the chair. Push your lower back into the chair so that you are ready to lift heavy weights. Brace yourself when seated, the angle at knee and hip should be about 90°.

2 Movement: vigorously straighten your legs and extend your toes, so that the force plate is resting on your toes. Most sporting activity involves extending the hip, knee and ankle in sequence (consider lifting, running, jumping, throwing and kicking).

3 Finishing position: sitting in the chair with the legs straight, knees and ankles extended.

MUSCLES USED

The muscles of the front of the thigh and the hips (rectus femoris, biceps femoris vastus [lateralis, intermedius and medialis], gluteus maximus and medius adductor [longus and magnus]).

BREATHING

Breathe in as you straighten your legs and push the pad away, and out as you relax and allow the pad to return to its starting position.

EXERCISE 27: FORWARD LUNGE

	M	F	M	F	M	F	M	F
Bodyweight kg	60	50	77	60	94	70	108	75
Novice	46	22	56	30	62	34	66	36
Club	55	26	66	36	73	41	79	43
Champion	68	32	82	44	81	50	98	53

PURPOSE

To strengthen and develop the muscles of the front of the upper leg and the hips.

KEY POSITIONS AND ACTIONS

1   Starting position: stand erect with the feet hip-width apart and the bar resting across the shoulders. Then take a large step forward with one foot; the alternative is to take a step backwards, and it is never a good idea to walk backwards with a heavy weight on your back when you cannot see where you are going. It does not matter which foot goes forward and which stays back as you will reverse the feet later.

2   Movement: bend the front knee, push the hips forward while keeping the trunk erect, so that your weight goes over the front foot with the thigh parallel to the floor. Then push back on the front foot and straighten the front leg.

3   Finishing position: finish with one foot in front of the other, with a hip-width distance between your two feet and both legs straight.

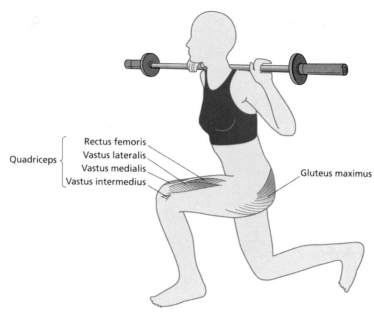

Quadriceps
- Rectus femoris
- Vastus lateralis
- Vastus medialis
- Vastus intermedius

Gluteus maximus

Figure 4.13 Muscles used in forward lunge

MUSCLES USED

The muscles of the front and back of the upper leg and the hips (rectus femoris and vastus [lateralis, medialis and intermedius] adductor magnus, biceps femoris and gluteus maximus).

BREATHING

Breathe out as you bend your legs so as to bring your front knee over your front foot, and breathe in as you straighten the legs to rise up again.

EXERCISE 28: STEP-UPS

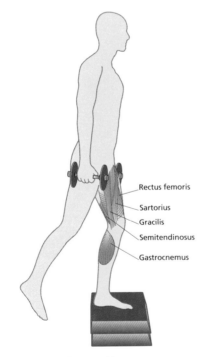

Figure 4.14 Muscles used in step-ups

Rectus femoris
Sartorius
Gracilis
Semitendinosus
Gastrocnemius

	M	F	M	F	M	F	M	F
Bodyweight kg	**60**	**50**	**77**	**60**	**94**	**70**	**108**	**75**
Novice	46	22	56	30	62	34	66	36
Club	55	26	66	36	73	41	79	43
Champion	68	32	82	44	91	50	98	53

PURPOSE

To strengthen and develop the muscles that extend the hip.

KEY POSITIONS AND ACTIONS

1   Starting position: stand erect with the bar resting across the back and facing a stable platform on which to step onto. It is important to stress that special care is needed to ensure your safety in this exercise. A gymnasium bench may be suitable to step up onto, but it must be stable as it could rotate as you step onto it, leaving you in a heap on the floor with

a weight falling onto you. It is also possible, when starting to perform this exercise, to over-balance backwards, so you will need to employ a spotter until you are confident in your balance.

2   Movement: place one foot onto the platform; it does not matter which one, as you will reverse the feet in a moment. Then vigorously drive upwards so that you are standing on the platform with both feet. Keep the feet facing forward and avoid twisting in either direction. You should lean forward very slightly with the head, so as not to overbalance backwards.

3   Finishing position: standing erect on the platform with the bar resting across the shoulders.

MUSCLES USED

The muscles of the front of the thigh and the hips (rectus femoris, vastus [lateralis, intermedius and medialis], gluteus maximus and medius, adductor [longus and magnus], semitendinosus and gastrocnemus).

BREATHING

Breathe in as you step up and out as you step down.

EXERCISE 29: BENCH PRESS

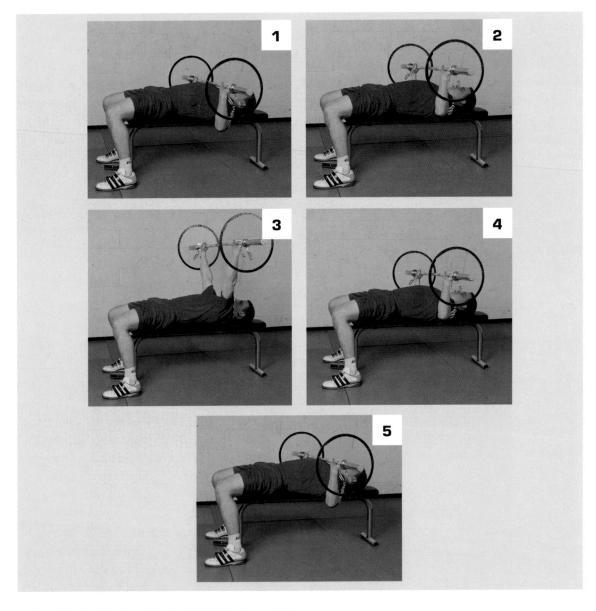

	M	F	M	F	M	F	M	F
Bodyweight kg	**60**	**50**	**77**	**60**	**94**	**70**	**108**	**75**
Novice	68	32	82	44	92	50	98	53
Club	81	39	97	53	108	60	116	63
Champion	101	48	122	66	135	75	145	79

PURPOSE

The greatest upper body exercise, developing and strengthening the muscles in the chest, shoulders and back of the upper arm.

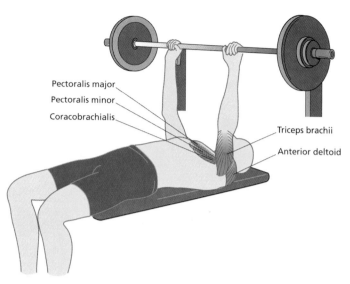

Pectoralis major

Pectoralis minor

Coracobrachialis

Triceps brachii

Anterior deltoid

Figure 4.15 Muscles used in the bench press

KEY POSITIONS AND ACTIONS

1   Starting position: it is essential to assume a stable position on the bench in order to start this exercise. Place your head, shoulders and hips firmly on the bench, with your feet either side of it. Gently arch your back so that there is daylight between your lower back and the bench. This puts the pectoralis major in a better mechanical position to contract. A spotter must be used to perform the exercise safely. They will lift the bar into the starting position after you have taken a palms-downward grip on the bar with hands slightly wider that shoulder-width apart. The bar should be directly over the shoulders.

2   Movement: bend your arms slowly so as to lower the bar slowly onto the chest (if you drop the bar onto your chest you can seriously injure yourself). This should be hard work with a heavy weight as you are slowing the descent of the bar to the chest. When the bar reaches the chest, touch it gently on the chest and then push it vigorously back out to arm's length so that it comes to rest over the shoulders again.

3   Finishing position: lying on your back on the bench with your head, shoulders and hips firmly on the bench and your feet planted on the floor on either side of it, maintaining the gentle arch described above. The bar held between the hands in a shoulder-width grip, palms downwards and over the shoulders.

MUSCLES USED

The muscles of the chest, shoulders and back, and the back of the upper arm (pectoralis major, pectoralis minor, anterior deltoid, latissimus dorsi, serratus anterior and triceps brachii [medial and long heads]).

BREATHING

Breathe in as you lower the bar under control to the chest and out as you drive the bar up to arm's length.

EXERCISE 30: INCLINED BENCH PRESS

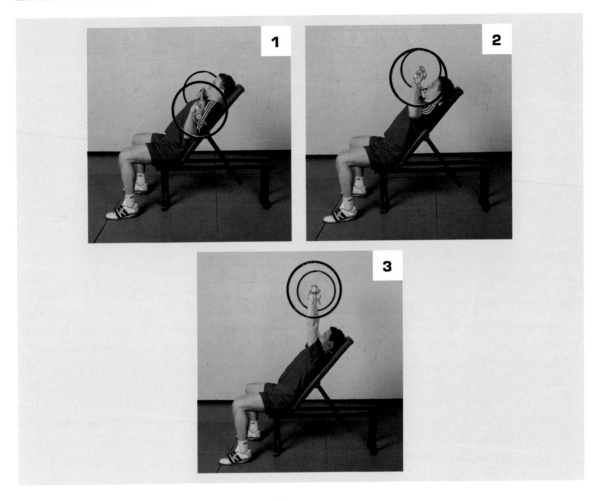

	M	F	M	F	M	F	M	F
Bodyweight kg	60	50	77	60	94	70	108	75
Novice	54	25	66	35	74	40	78	43
Club	65	30	78	42	86	48	93	51
Champion	81	39	98	53	108	60	116	64

PURPOSE

A large upper body exercise, developing and strengthening the muscles in the chest, shoulders and back of the upper arm.

KEY POSITION AND ACTIONS

1   Starting position: the inclined bench press is done in order to combine the work of the chest with the shoulders and the arms. The exact angle of the incline will depend on the specific reasons for doing the exercise. Athletic throwers in the shot, discus and hammer, for example, set the bench at 45 degrees in order to imitate throwing. Sit on the seat and lean back on the bench. Place the feet firmly on the

Triceps brachii

Anterior deltoid

Pectoralis major

Pectoralis minor

Figure 4.16 Muscles used in the inclined bench press

floor. Instruct your spotters to hand the bar across to you so that it is either at arm's length or on your chest, but be specific (see box below).

2 Movement: bend your arms slowly so as to lower the bar slowly onto the chest to a count of four. When the bar reaches the chest, touch it gently on the chest and then push it back out to arm's length so that it comes to rest over the shoulders again.

3 Finishing position: lying on your back on the bench with your head, shoulders and buttocks firmly on the bench and your feet planted on the floor on either side of it, maintaining the gentle arch described above. The bar held between the hands in a shoulder-width grip, palms downwards and over the shoulders.

MUSCLES USED

The muscles of the chest, shoulders and back, and the back of the upper arm (pectoralis major, pectoralis minor, anterior deltoid, latissimus dorsi, serratus anterior, corcobrachialis and triceps brachii).

BREATHING

Breathe in as you lower the bar under control to the chest and out as you drive the bar up to arm's length.

Communication

The command 'lift' should be given by the lifter to the spotter or spotters to get the bar to the starting position. 'My bar' indicates that the lifter has the bar in their control and the spotters should release their grip. The command 'rack' means they should return the bar to the rack after completion of the lift.

EXERCISE 31: LAT PULL DOWN

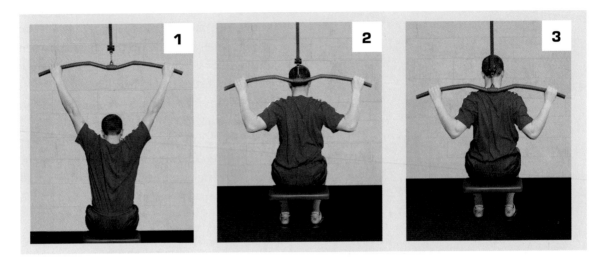

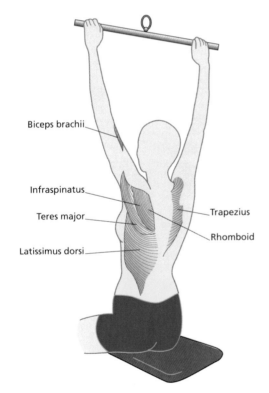

Figure 4.17 Muscles used in lat pull down

Biceps brachii

Infraspinatus

Teres major

Latissimus dorsi

Trapezius

Rhomboid

	M	F	M	F	M	F	M	F
Bodyweight kg	**60**	**50**	**77**	**60**	**94**	**70**	**108**	**75**
Novice	46	22	56	30	62	34	66	36
Club	55	26	66	36	73	41	79	43
Champion	68	32	82	44	81	50	98	53

PURPOSE

To strengthen the muscles of the front of the upper arm. and the middle back.

KEY POSITIONS AND ACTIONS

1. Starting position: adjust the machine so as to suit your size and shape. Sit on the bench with your feet on the floor and your knees under the pad. Take hold of the bar with a palms-downward grip slightly wider than shoulder-width apart.

2. Movement: pull the bar down and touch it gently across the shoulders behind the neck. Then relax under control so that the arms straighten and the bar returns to arm's length. In the last few years a number of athletes

have started bringing the bar down to their chest rather than to their backs, but this is highly dangerous, particularly with heavy weights, as it encourages the lifter to lean back, putting considerable pressure on the lower back and risking injury to it. Also, in this position athletes tend to pronate the hand, risking tennis elbow-type injuries. The reason given against bringing the bar down behind the head is that the athlete risks injury to the neck by striking it with the bar. However, all exercises need to be controlled and the athlete should slow the bar as it approaches the neck in order to eliminate the risk. Also, the athlete should keep the head up so that the bulk of the trapezius muscle is protecting the neck.

3   Finishing position: sitting upright on the bench with the feet firmly on the ground on either side. You should be holding the bar in a palms-downward grip, slightly wider than shoulder-width apart and the bar is resting across the shoulders.

MUSCLES USED

The muscles of the front of the upper arm and the middle back (biceps brachii, brachialis, brachioradialis, trapezius, rhomboid, infraspinatus, teres major and latissimus dorsi).

BREATHING

Breathe in as you draw the bar down to your shoulders and breathe out as you relax and let it rise up to arm's length.

EXERCISE 32: DUMBBELL FLIES

	M	F	M	F	M	F	M	F
Bodyweight kg	60	50	77	60	94	70	108	75
Novice	23	11	28	15	31	17	33	18
Club	28	12	33	18	37	21	40	22
Champion	34	16	41	22	41	25	49	27

Warning: It is very easy to injure yourself if you use a heavier weight than you can manage.

PURPOSE
To develop and strengthen the muscles of the chest.

KEY POSITIONS AND ACTIONS

1   Starting position: it is essential to assume a stable position on the bench in order to start this exercise. Place your head, shoulders and hips firmly on the bench, with your feet either side of it. Gently arch your back so that there is daylight between your lower back and the bench. Take the dumbbells from spotters so that you have a good grip on them. The dumbbells should be directly over the chest.

2   Movement: take the dumbbells out to the side of the chest so that you open up your chest. Control the movement carefully to avoid injury.

3   Finishing position: pull the two dumbbells together and back to the starting position over your chest.

MUSCLES USED
The muscles of the chest (pectoralis major, sternocostal head, latissimus dorsi, serratus anterior, clavicular head).

BREATHING
Breathe in as you lower the dumbbells under control to the side of the chest and breathe out as you raise the dumbbells to arm's length above the chest.

EXERCISE 33: GOOD MORNING

	M	F	M	F	M	F	M	F
Bodyweight kg	60	50	77	60	94	70	108	75
Novice	46	22	56	30	62	34	66	36
Club	55	26	66	36	73	41	79	43
Champion	68	32	82	44	81	50	98	53

Warning: This exercise will make a strong back stronger. It may cause serious injury to an untrained or unfit athlete.

PURPOSE

To develop and strengthen the muscles of the lower back, the hips and the back of the upper leg.

KEY POSITIONS AND ACTIONS

1   Starting position: stand erect with your feet hip-width apart. Place the bar across the shoulders so that you have a palms-downward grip on the bar, slightly wider than shoulder-width apart. Take a step out to the side with one foot so that you are more stable. Fix your eyes on a spot directly in front of you in order to keep your head up and your back straight.

2   Movement: keep your back very straight and flat and tilt forward from the hips to an angle of 45°. This will place a load on your lower back, which, if it is strong, will make it stronger, but which risks injury to a weak back. For this reason, always start this exercise with a very light weight and build up slowly.

3   Finishing position: standing bent forward, as in the picture 3. Feet wider than hip-width apart and with head up and eyes fixed directly in front.

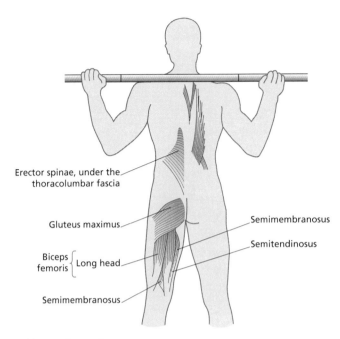

Erector spinae, under the thoracolumbar fascia

Gluteus maximus

Semimembranosus

Semitendinosus

Biceps femoris { Long head

Semimembranosus

Figure 4.18 Muscles used in good morning

MUSCLES USED

The muscles of the lower back, the hips and the back of the upper leg (erector spinae, gluteus maximus, semitendinosus, semimembranosus, biceps femoris [long and short heads]).

BREATHING

Breathe out as you bend forward under control and breath in as you vigorously straighten up.

EXERCISE 34: RUSSIAN TWIST

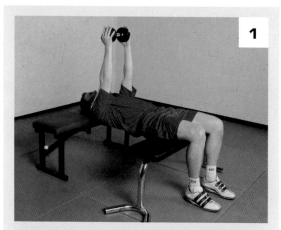

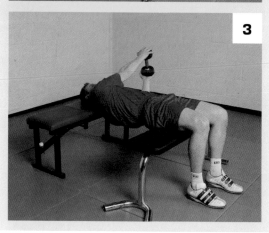

PURPOSE

To develop and strengthen the muscles of the front and side of the abdomen and trunk, used in activities such as athletic throwing. This exercise develops great core strength which is necessary in every sports discipline.

KEY POSITIONS AND ACTIONS

1   Starting position: place two benches parallel to each other, approximately 60cm apart. Sit on one bench and lean back so that your shoulders are resting on the other bench. Set your feet firmly on the floor and get a spotter to hold your knees down so that you avoid any unnecessary movement. Get another spotter to hand you a weightlifting disk to hold and hold it between both hands above your chest.

2   Movement: rotate your trunk so that you touch the weight on the floor on one side of the bench and then rotate the trunk the other way so that you touch the weight on the floor on the other side of the bench. If you have not done this exercise before you should feel a gentle stretch down the side or your trunk, but if you feel anything more than that, stop immediately.

3   Finishing position: sitting on one bench with the head and shoulders resting on the second bench and the weight at arm's length over the chest.

MUSCLES USED

Internal and external obliques.

BREATHING

Breathe out as you rotate your trunk to lower the weight under control and in as you vigorously turn to the other side.

EXERCISE 35: HYPEREXTENSIONS

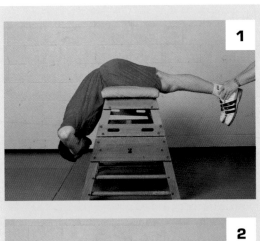

PURPOSE

To develop and strengthen the muscles of the lower back, hips and the back of the upper leg.

KEY POSITIONS AND ACTIONS

1   Starting position: lay on the pad in the centre of the machine and place your feet under the second pad at the back of the machine. Place your hands behind your head. This exercise can also be practised with a pommel horse, as shown, provided you have someone to hold your ankles. Ensure that you are well balanced before performing the hyperextension.

2   Movement: use the muscles of your lower back to pull your head up so that your body is straight from head to toe.

3   Finishing position: lying on the machine with your hips resting on the centre pad, your legs under the second pad and your body straight from head to toe.

MUSCLES USED

The muscles of the lower back and the back of the upper leg (longissimus thoracis, quadratus lumborum, iliocostalis lumborum, gluteus maximus and medius, semitendinosus, semi-membranosus, iliocostalis thoracis, erector spinae, intertransversarii laterales lumborum and biceps femoris).

BREATHING

Breathe in as you pull yourself up and breathe out as you lower yourself back to the starting position.

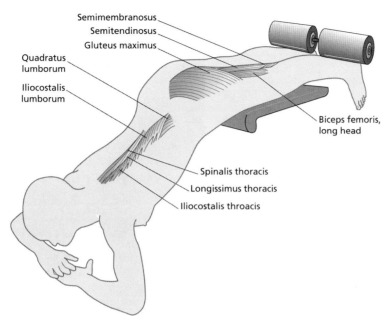

Semimembranosus
Semitendinosus
Gluteus maximus
Quadratus lumborum
Iliocostalis lumborum
Biceps femoris, long head
Spinalis thoracis
Longissimus thoracis
Iliocostalis throacis

Figure 4.19 Muscles used in hyperextensions

EXERCISE 36: DUMBBELL SIDE BEND

PURPOSE

To develop and strengthen the muscles at the side of the trunk, which are particularly important when lifting weights overhead.

KEY POSITIONS AND ACTIONS

1   Starting position: stand erect with the feet considerably wider than hip-width apart and the knees braced. Hold the dumbbell in one hand and place the other hand behind the head as shown. Push the hips slightly forward and lean to the side on which the dumbbell is held.

2   Movement: pull the head over to the opposite side to develop the trunk. It is essential that in performing this exercise the body is maintained in the lateral plane. By setting the hips slightly forward in the starting position, you are prevented from bending forwards. The knees must also

remain braced and the feet must be kept flat on the floor.

3 Finishing position: standing with feet considerably wider than hip-width apart. Leaning to one side with that hand behind the head and a weight in the other hand. Now transfer the dumbell to the other hand and reverse the exercise.

MUSCLES USED

This exercise develops the muscles on the side of the trunk and numerous other muscles which surround the mid-section (internal and external obliques) and the muscles of the lower back and spinal columns.

BREATHING

Breathe in as the weight is raised and out as you return to the starting position.

EXERCISE 37: BICEP CURL

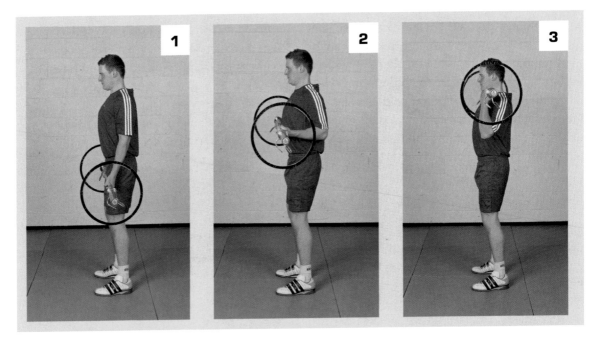

	M	F	M	F	M	F	M	F
Bodyweight kg	60	50	77	60	94	70	108	75
Novice	12	18	20	24	25	27	29	29
Club	19	21	29	29	34	33	39	35
Champion	30	26	41	36	49	41	54	43

PURPOSE

To strengthen, develop and increase the size of the muscles of the front of the upper arm.

KEY POSITIONS AND ACTIONS

1   Starting position: follow the instructions previously given on page 59 to get into the starting position. Take a palms-upward grip on the bar, slightly wider than shoulder-width apart. Stand up so that the bar is resting across the thighs.

2   Movement: take the elbows back and bring the bar up, close to the body to the top of the chest.

3   Finishing position: standing erect with feet hip-width apart and the bar held in a palms-upward grip at the top of the chest. Then lower bar down to the starting position under control until the arms are fully extended.

MUSCLES USED

The muscles on the front of the upper arm (biceps brachii, brachialis and brachioradialis).

BREATHING

Breathe in as you raise the bar and out as you lower it under control back to the starting position.

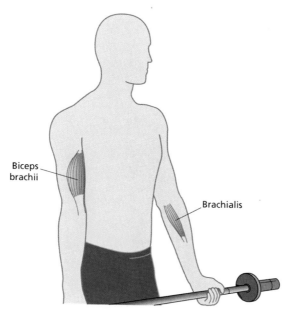

Figure 4.20 Muscles used in bicep curl

EXERCISE 38: TRICEP PRESS DOWN

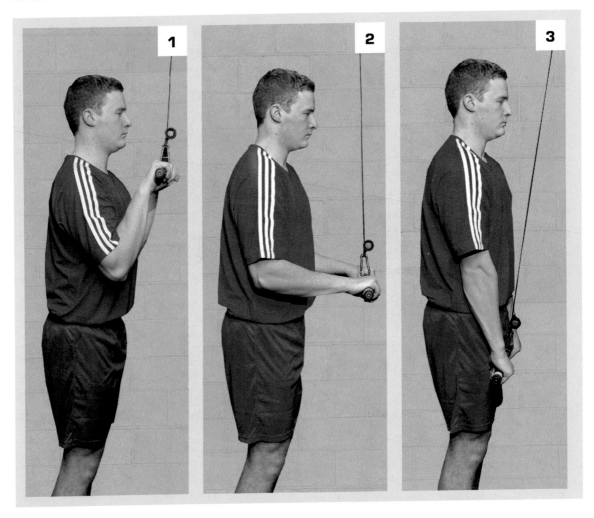

	M	F	M	F	M	F	M	F
Bodyweight kg	60	50	77	60	94	70	108	75
Novice	23	11	28	15	31	17	33	18
Club	28	12	33	18	37	21	40	22
Champion	34	16	41	22	47	25	49	27

PURPOSE

To strengthen and develop the muscles on the back of the upper arm.

KEY POSITIONS AND ACTIONS

1 Starting position: stand erect with feet hip-width apart. Take a palms-downward grip on the bar, closer than shoulder-width apart. Keep your body upright, shoulders back and the bar held at chest height.

2 Movement: keep the elbows as close together as possible as you straighten the arms and push the bar down towards your thighs.

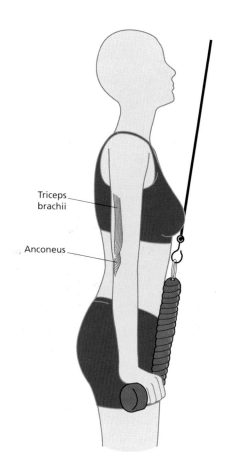

Triceps brachii

Anconeus

Figure 4.21 Muscles used in tricep press down

3 Finishing position: standing erect with feet hip-width apart. Palms-downward grip on the bar, narrower than shoulder-width apart and with straight arms holding the bar down against the thighs.

MUSCLES USED

The muscles on the back of the upper arm (triceps brachii [lateral, long and medial heads] and the anconeus).

BREATHING

Breathe in as you push the bar down and out as you relax and let the bar return to its top position.

EXERCISE: 39 WRIST CURL

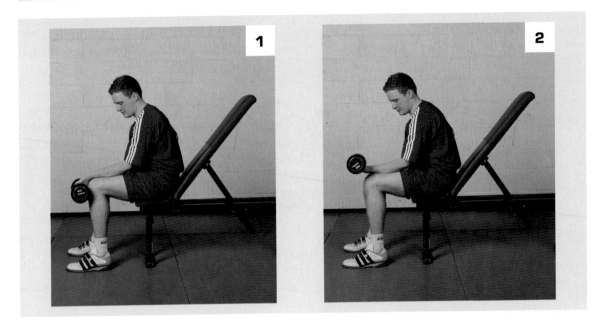

PURPOSE
To develop and strengthen the muscles of the forearm, which are essential to holding and gripping bars.

KEY POSITIONS AND ACTIONS
1 Starting position: sit on a bench holding a bar in a palms-upward grip, with your forearms resting along your thighs and your hands projecting beyond your legs.
2 Movement: relax your forearms so that the wrists bend down. Then draw the hands back towards you so that they pull the bar up.

3 Finishing position: sitting on a bench holding a bar in a palms-upward grip, with your forearms resting along your thighs and your hands pulled towards you.

MUSCLES USED
The muscles of the front of the forearm (flexor carpi radialis, palmaris longus, flexor digitorum superficialis, flexor digitorum profundus).

BREATHING
Breathe in as you raise the bar and out as you lower the bar under control.

Flexor carpi radialis

Palmaris longus

Flexor digitorum superficialis and profundus

Flexor carpi ulnaris

Flexor digitorum superficialis, covering flexor digitorum profundus

Flexor pollicis longus

Figure 4.22 Muscles used in wrist curl

EXERCISE 40: REVERSE WRIST CURL

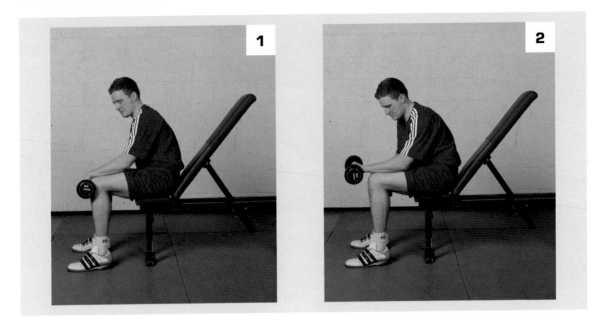

PURPOSE

To strengthen and develop the muscles on the back of the forearm.

KEY POSITIONS AND ACTIONS

1　Starting position: sit on a bench holding a bar in a palms-downward grip, with your forearms resting along your thighs and your hands projecting beyond your legs.

2　Movement: relax your forearms so that the wrists bend down. Then draw the hands back towards you so that they pull the bar up as far as they can.

3　Finishing position: sitting on a bench holding a bar in a palms-downward grip, with your forearms resting along your thighs and your hands pulled up towards you.

MUSCLES USED

The muscles on the back of the forearm (extensor carpi radialis [longus and brevis] extensor digitorum, extensor digiti minimi and extensor carpi ulnaris).

BREATHING

Breathe in as you raise the bar and out as you lower it under control.

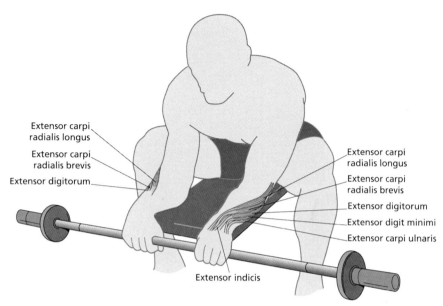

Figure 4.23 Muscles used in reverse wrist curl

QUESTIONS

Level 2

Q.1. It has been said that twice as many athletes overtrain as undertrain. Design a session plan of exercises designed to maximally increase the allround leg strength of a young athlete committed to becoming a strength athlete.

Q.2. It has been said that twice as many athletes overtrain as undertrain. Design a session plan of exercises designed to maximally increase the allround arm strength of a young athlete committed to becoming a strength athlete.

Q.3. It has been said that twice as many athletes overtrain as undertrain. Design a session plan of exercises designed to maximally increase the allround core strength of a young athlete committed to becoming a strength athlete.

Q.4. Describe the movement in the squat clean with reference to the five key positions.

Q.5. Describe the movement in the back squat with particular reference to the depth of the squat.

Q.6. List three popular exercises used by strength athletes that you would strongly discourage an inexperienced athlete from attempting.

Level 3

Q.1. Describe the movement in the squat snatch with reference to the five key positions. Explain the reasons for each of the five key positions.

Q.2. Describe the surface position of the muscles used in the upright rowing exercise. Name those muscles that you are able to.

Q.3. Describe the movement in the bench press. Explain the reasons why it is essential to keep both feet firmly planted on the ground during the execution of the lift. Explain the consequences of moving the grip wider and narrower.

Q.4. Some people have recently taken to performing the lat pull down by pulling the bar down in front of their head rather than behind their head. Explain why this is dangerous.

Q.5. List the muscles used in the performance of the press, and their surface position.

Q.6. Explain the movement of the forward lunge, the key teaching points and the muscles used.

Level 4

Q.1. Describe the way to get into the starting position, the movement and the finishing position of the bent forward rowing exercise.

Q.2. The front squat is a simple exercise, but the fine points of technique are essential in order to avoid serious chronic injuries as a result of lifting large numbers of repetitions with very heavy weights over a number of years. Set out as many of these finer points of technique as necessary to avoid injury.

Q.3. Explain the similarities and differences between the front squat and the back squat. Would you ever use both in one schedule?

Q.4. Many athletes find the squat snatch difficult to perform due to a lack of flexibility. Where do they feel this lack of flexibility and what exercises can they perform in order to improve their flexibility so that they can perform this exercise?

Q.5. Explain the advantages and disadvantages of performing some lifts from the hang position or from blocks.

Q.6. Name the factor that determines success or failure in both the snatch and clean.

// BIBLIOGRAPHY

Baechle, T.R. and Earle, R.W. (2008) *Essentials of Strength Training and Conditioning*, USA. Human Kinetics Publishers

Baechle, T.R. and Groves, B.R. (1998) *Weight Training: Steps to Success* (2nd edn), USA. Human Kinetics Publishers

Bean, A. (2003) *The Complete Guide to Sports Nutrition* (4th edn), London. A&C Black

Bean, A. (2007) *Food for Fitness* (3rd edn), London. A&C Black

Behm, D. G., et al. (2005) 'Trunk muscle electromyographic activity with unstable and unilateral exercises', *Journal of Strength and Conditioning Research* 19(1): 193–201

Behm, D.G., Faigenbaum, A.D., Falk, B. and Klentrou, P. (2008) 'Canadian Society for Exercise Physiology Position Paper: Resistance Training in Children and Adolescents', *Applied Physiology, Nutrition and Metabolism* 33(3): 547–561

Bompa, T.O. and Cornacchia, L.J. (1998) *Serious Strength Training*, USA. Human Kinetics Publishers

Chaitow, L. (1999) *Muscle Energy Techniques* (2nd edn), London. Churchill Livingstone Elsevier

Dick, F.W. (2003) *Sports Training Principles*, London. A&C Black

Faigenbaum, A.D., Kraemer, W.J., Cahill, B., Chandler, J., Dziados, J., Elfrink, L.D., et al. (1996) 'Youth Resistance Training: Position Statement Paper and Literature Review', *Strength & Conditioning Journal* 18: 62–75

Faigenbaum, A.D. and Westcott, W.L. (2000) *Strength and Power for Young Athletes*, USA. Human Kinetics Publishers

Fleck, S.J. and Kraemer, W.J. (2004) *Designing Resistance Training Programs*, USA. Human Kinetics Publishers

Fleck, S.J. and Kraemer, W.J. (2007) *Optimising Strength Training*, USA. Human Kinetics Publishers

Howley, E.T. and Franks, B.D. (2007) *Fitness Professional's Handbook*, USA. Human Kinetics Publishers

Kendall, F. (1993) *Muscles Testing and Function; With Posture and Pain* (4th edn), USA. Lippincott Williams & Wilkins

King, I. and Schuler, L. (2003) *Men's Health: The Book of Muscle*, USA. Rodale

Marsh, G.E. (2007) *Stronger and Fitter for Life* (1st edn), London. A&C Black

McArdle, W. D., Katch, F. I. and Katch, V. L. (1986) *Exercise Physiology*, Led & Febiger

McGill, S. (2006) *Ultimate Back Fitness and Performance* (3rd edn), Canada. Backfitpro Inc

National Strength Conditioning Association (2006) *Strength Training*, USA. Human Kinetics Publishers

Newton, H. (2006) *Explosive Lifting for Sports*, USA. Human Kinetics Publishers

Poliquin, C. (2006a) *Modern Trends in Strength Training* (4th edn), Poliquin Performance Centres

Poliquin, C. (2006b) *Poliquin Principles: Successful Methods for Strength and Mass Development*, Poliquin Performance Centres

Rippetoe, M. and Kilgore, L. (2005) *Starting Strength*, USA. Aasgard Company

Rippetoe, M. and Kilgore, L. (2006) *Practical Programming for Strength Training*, USA. Aasgard Company

Sahrmann, S. (2002) *Diagnosis and Treatment of Movement Impairment Syndromes*, USA. Mosby

Schmidt, R.A. and Wrisberg, C.A. (2000) *Motor Learning and Performance* (2nd edn), USA. Human Kinetics Publishers

Siff, M. (1993) *Supertraining* (1st edn), USA. Supertraining Institute

Silva III, J.M. (1990) 'An Analysis of the Training Stress Syndrome in Competitive Athletics', *Journal of Applied Sports Psychology*, 2:5–20

Stratton, G., Jones, M., Fox, K.R., Tolfrey, K., Harris, J., Maffulli, N., Lee, M. and Frostick, S.P. (2004) 'BASES Position Statement on Guidelines for Resistance Exercise in Young People', *Journal of Sports Sciences* (4):383–390

Thibaudeau, C. (2006) *The Black Book of Training Secrets (Enhanced Edition)*, F. Lepine

Tippet, S.R. and Voight, M.R. (1995) *Functional Progressions for Sports Rehabilitation*, USA. Human Kinetics Publishers

Voight et al. (eds) (2007) *Musculoskeletal Interventions*, USA. McGraw-Hill

Vossen et al. 'Comparison of Dynamic Push-Up Training and Plyometric Push-Up Training on Upper-Body Power and Strength', *The Journal of Strength and Conditioning Research* (14)3:248–253

Wilmore, J. H. and Costill, D. L. (1994) *Physiology of Sport and Exercise*, USA. Human Kinetics Publishers

Zatsiorsky, V. (1995) *The Science and Practice of Strength Training*, USA. Human Kinetics Publishers

INDEX

KU-203-140

Contents

A Levels – The Essential Guide is also available in accessible formats for people with any degree of visual impairment. The large print edition and E-Book (with accessibility features enabled) are available from Need2Know. Please let us know if there are any special features you require and we will do our best to accommodate your needs.

First published in Great Britain in 2012 by
Need2Know
Remus House
Coltsfoot Drive
Peterborough
PE2 9BF
Telephone 01733 898103
Fax 01733 313524
www.need2knowbooks.co.uk

All Rights Reserved
© Need 2 Know Ltd. 2012
SB ISBN 978-1-86144-264-2
Cover photograph: Dreamstime

ANDOVER COLLEGE

059585

A LEVELS

WITHDRAWN The Essential Guide

Charlotte
Evans

ANDOVER COLLEGE

STUDY
CENTRE

2A CAREERS 371.30281

Introduction

With the A level exams, now known as A1 and A2 exams, the first thing you must do is accept that these exams – the course of study and the related pressures – are absolutely worth pursuing.

It goes without saying that good A level results are essential for entrance into higher education at the vast majority of colleges and universities. If you have plans for a career, then A level success, more than likely, is a crucial component for your future.

Another thing to consider, perhaps, is that A levels, following on from GCSE studies, can offer some really refreshing learning experiences. Although the components of most exams and courses have changed in the last several years, studying for A levels affords a rewarding experience academically. The courses offer more opportunity for independent study. In many instances, the programme of study for A levels can be a 'taster' for the university experience that follows as the next stage in your education.

The second thing you need to accept is the notion that you are probably approaching the A level experience with a solid skill set and good working knowledge of your chosen subjects. At the same time, though, these skills and this knowledge base has to be expanded and perhaps even somewhat remoulded for you to succeed at A level.

The purpose of this book is to help you and your parents reconcile yourself to what the A level experience may mean; at the same time, it is designed to help you prepare to be the best supporter of yourself through the A level experience.

Our goal is to present you with a no-nonsense strategy to support yourself from the very beginning of your A level experience, starting with subject selection and the important decision to study A levels, right the way through to results day, and all that it entails.

A note to parents

As parents, your support through A level and A level study can, and often really should, take on a variety of forms. For the most part, you should probably trust that your child has the skills and knowledge to handle much if not all of the academic demands set upon them. If they struggle academically, they may well also have direct access to resources that will allow them to get the help they need. Chances are, that you are going to be needed in other ways to support your child's needs outside of the classroom and help them deal not necessarily with the purely academic demands, but rather with issues like stress, time management, and even issues with their preparation to move on to the next stage of their life – beyond secondary school.

How to use this book

The best way to use this book involves a two-step process. The first step is really the crucial one. You should set aside the time to read the book from cover to cover, the benefit of this is that you will have the chance to observe the range of ideas, suggestions and strategies offered within its pages. The second step is for you to read this book as a guide book, accessing information that is relevant to a particular issue you might be experiencing.

Chapter One

A Levels: What Are They and Why Are They Important?

What are A levels?

A level is the common term used to refer to the GCE Advanced Level Examinations. GCE stands for General Certificate of Education.

Basically, the Advanced Level General Certificate of Education, or A level, is a qualification awarded to those who complete a two-year course of study and submit to standardised testing in chosen subjects.

Who uses them?

A levels are qualifications, first and foremost. They are, therefore, used by institutions of higher education to assess the academic abilities and overall suitability of candidates interested in study. They are also used by employers in certain situations.

These qualifications are offered by educational institutions in specific locations – England, Wales, Northern Ireland, and in certain institutions in Scotland.

Note that the Scottish Qualifications Certificate Higher and Advanced Higher are the standardised tests usually taken by students in Scotland, rather than A levels.

'A levels are used by institutions of higher education to assess the academic abilities and overall suitability of candidates interested in study.'

Although they are generally recognised as reputable qualifications around the world, it is in these locations that they are deemed standard for assessment.

How are they graded?

A levels are broken down into two units. The first of these units is the AS level and the second is the A2 level.

With the exception of certain natural science subjects, each of these two units are broken down into two modules, four in total.

For each module, you will be assessed either with a coursework assignment or with an examination. If you think about it, it's very much like GCSEs in that respect. For each assignment, however, you will receive a grade that is both a numerical grade (a score out of so many points) and a letter grade.

Most assessments are done as written examinations. Coursework can also be applied throughout the two years of study. Coursework tends to consist of things such as essays, performances and experiments.

Whereas coursework is generally graded by a teacher then sent to an external examination board to be checked for consistency in the grading, written exams are graded by third parties outside of your child's school.

Some subjects, such as art or drama, require a practical examination as you probably know.

When do AS and A2 exams take place?

Written examinations take place either in January to February or in May to June.

Because A levels are standardised tests and used to assess students across several regions, it is necessary that certain procedures are followed to ensure that all students have equal opportunity to perform.

A level exams are conducted according to very strict guidelines. Students must sit in silence and they must focus on their own paper.

What do grades mean?

To pass A level examinations, you must obtain a grade E or above. The highest grade, as of 2010, is an A* grade. Prior to 2010, the highest grade was simply an A.

A level grades range from E to A*, with A* being the highest. There are, however, specific criteria that must be met to achieve each of these individual grades.

Raw marks are applied to written examination papers according to a Uniform Marking Scale, or UMS.

This UMS is used to determine the numerical scoring criteria for different grades. In most instances, if a student scores an average of 90% across A2 modules they are awarded an A*. A score of 80+% is also an A grade, 70-79% offers a B grade, 60-69% is a C grade, 50-59% is a D grade, and 40-49% is the bottom pass E grade.

Grades are also converted to so-called UCAS points. AS levels receive up to 60 points for an A grade, reducing by 10 for each grade lower.

What about UCAS points and university application? Well, each grade is equivalent to a number of points that meet the criteria for your university application. Your AS level will also offer you UCAS points of up to 60 for an A grade, reducing by 10 per grade below.

It is based on the actual breakdown of the modules and the grades that your final grade will be determined.

'To pass A level examinations, you must obtain a grade E or above.'

Why are they important?

Assuming you have plans to go into higher education, A levels are crucial. Without A levels, assuming you have been educated in the regions we mentioned above – the ones that accept A levels as a primary form of standardised testing – you are unlikely to get a university placement.

Why is it important for parents to be involved in the A level process?

Most parents have mixed feelings seeing their children under pressure. Still, they know there are times when a) pressure is unavoidable and b) it is in your best interests. This is the situation with A levels as with most other exams and stressful situations that relate to opportunities for success.

There are specific types of support that you will probably want from your parents throughout your A level experience, though.

Besides the obvious, that include food and shelter, room and board, you may want to have your parents available as a sounding board for some of the decisions you have to make (e.g. what subjects to study at AS and A2 level, what subjects to drop at A2, which university courses you should apply for etc.)

'The key to having your parents support you effectively, is to communicate your wants and needs.'

You may also want your parents on board to help you manage your schedule, prioritise, and create an effective balance in your life between work and school.

More than likely you are also going to want your parents to be understanding when you are under pressure, working hard to meet deadlines and revising hard for your exams.

The key to having your parents support you effectively, though, is to communicate your wants and needs. Keep the lines of communication open. Let them know how you are feeling when you are struggling but do so in a non-confrontational way. Don't be afraid to ask for help.

Why your parents may have a hard time understanding A levels

Granted there are a few books, websites and articles out there that go some way to helping students and their parents understand the current A level exams and why they are important. Despite the available information, though, your parents may still have a hard time understanding the system for this level of study.

Perhaps the most obvious reason for this struggle is good old-fashioned change. The A levels have been around for a while but they have changed continuously and, in recent times, have even changed quite dramatically. Parents looking back to their own experience of A levels will certainly be referencing an experience that is very different from what you will be going through. Anything your parents have told you about their experiences is unlikely to be all that relevant to yours. There is also the changing nature of these exams and the respective study courses. Most people approaching the A levels for the first time have no real point of reference.

Your parents don't have much of a reference point, either. Their best point of reference is probably going to be their recollection of A levels several decades ago. If you have a parent who is also a teacher – someone who has experience teaching A level courses – your parent might be something of an exception. However, even with an exception like this, there are many issues.

For one, because parents (all adults, in fact) have to remember their own experiences or rely on experiences from others in their family or circle of friends, they are looking at the A level process from a perspective that may not even be relevant for you.

If their A level experience was several years ago, then they have no context for understanding the modern A level exam unless you have older siblings.

Even in the last ten years, though, the A level exams have changed. In fact, it's pretty safe to say that they change at least every couple of years. There was also the rather dramatic change from two-year study programmes to the system for AS and A2 levels, breaking down those two years into single-year courses.

Now, if parents are relying on the experience of people whose children have taken their A levels within the last few years, at least the AS and A2 problem is out of the way.

You will want to communicate regularly with your parents, to help them keep up to date with the challenges you are facing, with the worries you are experiencing, and the challenges you are overcoming.

'Most people approaching the A levels for the first time have no real point of reference.'

Consider making it a habit to set aside time to talk to your parents at least once a week specifically about your A level experience – your course load, your goals, your questions/issues, your career plans, your university applications, your predicted grades . . . anything.

What can you do to familiarise yourself with A levels and what they involve?

Before you start your A level studies, you are going to want to find out as much as you can about what they will entail. Although your parents may not be the best source of information on what to expect, there are plenty of useful resources you can access in order to answer questions about the A level process.

For one thing, you can certainly ask a family friend or other relatives about what the AS and A2 courses are like in general, and get some good feedback. There is still the problem of knowing how you will react to the experience and what you will get from it, but talking to other students is definitely a step in the right direction.

The problem with this source of information, though, is that it is pretty diverse and not exactly representative. One student might excel at A level, thriving on the pressure, picking all the right subjects. Another might find that they struggle to manage the higher level of expectations; that they've ended up with subjects that don't actually interest them; or that they simply don't enjoy the higher education experience that A level studies still afford most students.

You can certainly access books like this one – and we have listed some resources you can use to get some idea of what A levels may be like in the help list.

You should remember though, that it is almost impossible to know exactly how an individual is going to react because everyone reacts differently to the experience.

But what do you do? How can you go about understanding and even anticipating how you will deal with A levels?

Because the A level experience is something teachers have a lot of knowledge about – probably teaching many different types of students – they may be one of the best sources of information.

If you are really worried about trying to anticipate how you will cope with A levels – what problems you might experience, what grades you might expect, and what strategies might help you through your courses – your teacher should actually be a good resource for general information. Keep in mind, that correlating experiences is not easy or often even practical. We all have different strengths (intellectual, psychological, personal), and this needs to be taken into account.

Of course, we've just implied how difficult it may be to successfully understand what you are going to experience at A level. If it's so difficult, near impossible, what, then, is the goal of this book?

As we suggested earlier, this book sets out to help you gain a solid knowledge of A level to support yourself. You may not be able to really gauge how studying for A levels is going to affect you overall, but you can go some way to anticipating issues and you can also do a lot to be proactive about managing them.

'Preparing will help you understand where you want to go.'

Why preparation is the key to A level success

Preparing for A levels – having a plan ahead of time for what you want to study and how you want to use your A level qualifications – will help you to work through challenging aspects of A level study. Preparing will help you understand where you want to go. Knowing where you want to go, you will be better able to focus throughout your A level studies. The reward for focus will be positive, excellent results.

Summing Up

- A levels are standardised tests used to assess the ability of students in England, Wales, Northern Ireland and parts of Scotland.

- The purpose of the A levels is to provide a way to assess how well a student performs in a given subject relative to peers at an advanced level.

- A levels are crucial for university entrance and can be important for obtaining employment after completion of sixth form.

- You need to invest yourself in the A level process because a) these are important examinations having a dramatic impact on your future, and b) there are numerous challenges to overcome during a typical A level experience.

Chapter Two

How to Prepare for A Levels Before Year 12

Why you should prepare for A levels ahead of time

Many students and their parents wonder what they can do to prepare for important times of life. With A levels, there is no exception. This is not only an important time in your education and in your life, it is really one of those times in which you, and even your parents, can feel rather helpless.

After all, no one can step into the exam room with you and hold your hand. It's unlikely anyone is going to micromanage your study schedule, your exam preparations, or your focus on A level coursework and exam work.

By the time you are in Year 12, you are expected to have sufficient motivation coupled with sufficient skills and knowledge to manage your own workload for school.

A common question for secondary school students, though, is, 'What can we do to prepare for exams?' Obviously A level and GCSE exams are the primary consideration and the real focus of these questions. So, what can you do to prepare for A level exams before you actually begin studying for them?

Although you may have found a few strategies yourself while preparing for GCSE exams, in this chapter we will offer a few suggestions on how you can prepare for your A level exams effectively and ahead of time.

'By the time you are in Year 12, you are expected to have sufficient **motivation coupled with sufficient skills and knowledge** to manage your own workload for school.'

Helping yourself to enjoy school

For this first suggestion, we could say something like, 'Make sure you are happy in the school you are at' but what we have allows a slightly wider scope for discussion.

When you made the transition from primary school to secondary school, it was important that you (and your parents) made an educated determination about what type of learning environment you were going into and what type of learning environment was going to be most supportive of your needs.

Take, for example, if you were enthusiastic and driven in music or sports. Although you may not want to limit the scope of your education by going to a school that specifically specialised in music or sports coaching and education, you and your parents would probably consider your interests in these areas when looking at school options.

'Most schools demonstrate strengths in a particular area or perhaps a handful of areas.'

If they knew that the opportunity to indulge a love of music or sports would help make you want to go to school every day, your parents would be quite open to choosing a school where this kind of indulgence would be supported. At the same time, if you particularly enjoyed studying languages or sciences, you may assess secondary school options with your parents based on the programme of teaching in these areas.

Most schools demonstrate strengths in a particular area or perhaps a handful of areas. Very few schools are excellent all round with academics and extracurricular activities. Finding the right school may require some compromises, although it is undoubtedly important to your future success.

One of the things you can do to help yourself prepare for A levels is communicate with your parents and teachers about how you are feeling at school. If you are unhappy with any aspect of school leading up to A levels, consider your options for improving the situation. Improvement may also involve transferring to a new school. Given the break between GCSE and A level, it is not a bad time to make a transition if you feel you would be happier at another school.

If you enjoy your school and are looking forward to the next two years of study – excellent. But take advantage of this position and give yourself opportunity to stay on top of any issues that may arise. Try to communicate openly with parents and teachers about any issues that come up. You may be worried about the subject selection at A level, for instance, and want to clarify ahead of time that you are going to be able to study the subjects you want at A level.

Accepting the importance of schoolwork and homework

Although you want to have a broad range of experiences through school, including extracurricular interests, friendships, or other perks as necessary; once you are in secondary school (at the very latest) you should have started to realise the benefits and the importance of hard work and perseverance.

You should have started to recognise your role in the larger scheme of things, especially as you worked your way through GCSE. You should have begun to appreciate that the work you do at secondary school, at GCSE and then at A level, is the basis for an all-important bridge between childhood and adulthood.

The higher up in school you go, the easier it will be to realise this connection. Hopefully, by the time you were going through your GCSEs, in Years 10 and 11, you had a fairly solid grasp on the relative importance of school.

If not, if you find it hard to put schoolwork high on your priority list, consider sitting down with your careers advisor or classroom teacher and talking about the problems and the reasons why you find it hard to consider schoolwork important.

Many schools operate a mentor system, at least for A level, so by Year 12, you should have a teacher who is directly concerned with your wellbeing and academic development. If you feel you are struggling to maintain your focus on schoolwork leading up to or during your A level studies, consider reaching out to one or two people who work closely with you to open a conversation about any possible underlying issues.

Many GCSE and A level students appear to have issues engaging in learning when they are struggling to understand some of the material they are working on or otherwise finding that they are uninterested in what they are learning.

'The work you do at secondary school, at GCSE and then at A level, is the basis for an all-important bridge between childhood and adulthood.'

Although something as drastic as a course change would be a last resort, it is important to make sure that you are appropriately challenged by your work at school – not too intimidated or too bored with it.

Accessing help and support

If you find yourself struggling through secondary school, consider going to your parents or otherwise finding a tutor or mentor to help you with your weaker subjects. Don't be afraid to approach a subject teacher.

Ideally this should be done prior to starting either GCSEs or A levels.

'It is important to make sure that you are appropriately challenged by your work at school – not too intimidated or too bored with it.'

Another option, if you are struggling, is to reach out to any friends or family with older children, who are at least a year or two above you. Fostering a kind of buddy system or big brother/sister programme can work, too, giving you someone to go to with questions about specific concepts or assignments you are struggling with.

Homework

As a general rule, you should be setting aside at least a couple of hours a day to get homework and some revision done during the two years you are studying for your A level grades. Doing this demonstrates that you take your schoolwork seriously and regard it as a priority. Give yourself that reminder to stay on target.

Exploring extracurricular and community activities

It is sometimes pointed out that there are at least five developmental areas for human beings – behavioural, cognitive, social, emotional and physical. This applies to teenagers too, and explains the notion that everyone, even adults, should aim to have a balanced life.

In other words, and aside from making school a priority, it is important to give yourself opportunities to develop socially, emotionally, physically, and even behaviourally, to support cognitive development at school.

Find the right balance

To start maintaining a balanced life and to help yourself mature properly, consider identifying and pursuing a number of extracurricular activities. In addition to helping you create a balance, meaningful pursuit of extracurricular activities can also lead to a very attractive-looking CV and, ultimately, a better university placement or job placement.

Schemes such as the Duke of Edinburgh Award offer excellent opportunities for you to learn important skills to be self-sufficient and effective.

Participation in sporting activities can also be a wonderful opportunity for you to achieve balance, too. Not to mention, regular participation in sports or exercise programmes can improve overall health and even produce greater focus.

Look into extracurricular activities or projects offered by your school as well as by your local community centre. Sit down with your parents and discuss what activities you are interested in and what activities might be beneficial for things such as university applications and CVs, as well as for things such as relaxation and socialisation during the two-year A level experience.

Keeping yourself motivated

- Write down three to five things you've done well each day, before you go to bed.

- List ten things you can do in a day to build your confidence, then work to make these things daily habits.

- Learn something new, as learning new things will increase your overall confidence level.

- Remember that confidence comes from taking risks. Don't be afraid to take risks, even when you don't yet feel confident in yourself. Confidence will come slowly.

- Work to appreciate who you are and what you already have.

- Start repeating affirmations every day, when you wake up and before you go to sleep.

'As a general rule, you should be setting aside at least a couple of hours a day to get homework and some revision done during the two years you are studying for your A level grades.'

Taking charge of your future and learning to prioritise before A levels

Reasons to plan

It might seem a little far-fetched, but as you are planning and preparing for your A levels, it is a good time to think, if you haven't already, about what you want to do with your life. Granted, nothing you decide or plan for at A level, or at any other point in your life, is set in stone. That is perhaps one of the great things about having access to a good education – you have options. But just because you have options, and you want to have flexibility, that doesn't mean to say that you can't plan thoroughly and organise yourself for a year, two years, even five or ten years ahead.

It might seem a long way off at A level, but it is only a couple of years before you are going to be looking to establish a career for yourself. Or a good job at least.

'Having a plan and being a focused, purposeful person is going to help you as an adult. And it can make your A level experience that much easier, too.'

Having a plan and being a focused, purposeful person is going to help you as an adult. And it can make your A level experience that much easier, too.

Creating a plan

So planning is a good thing. But how exactly do you 'plan' your life in a functional way?

The important detail of any plan is the content – the quality of the goals that you set for yourself.

Regardless of how you decide to lay out your plan, you should look to discuss your goals in a logical way.

Because the best plans are going to cover all areas of your life, consider mapping out some goals for yourself in the following areas:

- In your family life – Your family is your strongest link to the past and the group of people most likely to be there for you in the future. Throughout your A level experience, you are probably going to rely on your parents quite a bit

22

for moral support. Although it may seem that you don't have to work on this much, you should still develop a plan to reinforce a positive relationship with your family as you work on laying out your future plans.

- In your career – Your actual career might seem a bit of a way off, as we have said, but you are probably not unknown to your school's careers advisor by this point. The reason is simple: it is not that long before you will have to be thinking about your career, just as you are now thinking about your A level options and grades. And the more preparation you can do, the better. You should at least be thinking about your career options at this point, and being ready to establish a general direction. You may have to choose a university and degree course. One of the factors – perhaps the biggest factor – informing this decision, is going to be your career interests. What do you want to do? What careers sound appealing to you? Think about establishing some work experience placements for yourself either to clarify your career aspirations or rule out some options. Consider your work schedule for school to figure out when it makes the most sense to be timing these placements.

- In your intellectual development – Knowledge is food for the mind and spirituality is good for the soul. You don't have to be a straight A student to enjoy learning new things, particularly when you're an adult. But it is often really useful to be open-minded about learning new things and exploring interests that might be thought of as 'intellectual' or 'academic' based. Although you are probably taking care of most of your 'intellectual' development simply by being in school, one thing that is very easy to do is reading around your subjects at A level. Reading anything, actually, for fun or for habit, is good. Think about setting up a study programme abroad or something similar for your summer vacation. You could simply join your local library and commit to reading one book a month or every two weeks, depending on what your schedule allows. Numerous studies have shown that actively exercising the mind improves memory and helps to prevent against degenerative diseases of old age, such as Alzheimer's. Your mind is like a muscle. You need to exercise it regularly to keep it in shape – you'll gain yet more confidence in yourself and your abilities as you test yourself in this way.

'Think about establishing some work experience placements for yourself either to clarify your career interests or rule out some options.'

- In your spiritual development – You don't have to be religious to be spiritual, but finding meaning in life and feeling that you are 'giving back' somewhat, can be very helpful and very rewarding as you are working through your A level experience. Spirituality is really more about being in touch with the world at large as a conscious being. It can be something you pursue independently, such as undertaking some kind of community service, or finding a volunteer opportunity that is meaningful to you can give you a nice outlet and escape from the other demands in your life. Whether it's meditating to stay calm for exams or volunteering at a local animal shelter, think about finding something to do that can bring you more in touch with who you are, increasing your self-awareness in a way that gives back and feels rewarding.

- In terms of your physical wellbeing – Teenagers in particular, as you are probably aware, have a lot of baggage associated with their appearance. But the truth is, most people have this baggage, and it is not exactly healthy for self-esteem. One way to boost your self-esteem and be healthy at the same time, is to make a practice of eating a healthy, balanced diet and establishing a reasonable schedule for physical activity. Exercise is, among other things, a great way to relax, boost your mood and reduce stress. It's a very useful tool during your A level experience. To begin work on your physical wellbeing, examine how you live at present. Do you eat enough fruit and vegetables per day? Do you drink enough water? When it comes to exercise, find an activity that isn't too strenuous. The best type of exercise for maintaining health is aerobic exercise – walking, swimming, jogging – and this is generally what you should start out doing anyway. Establish a schedule to address your physical wellbeing as a final aspect of developing yourself. You can tackle two goals in one by playing a team sport through your school or local club, for example.

Going through each of these categories, you can make plans for yourself for your A level experience and beyond. What you will find early on is that having clear goals – a clear direction – is a great way to be in control of your life. And with control comes benefits such as reduced stress and a general sense of confidence that will also serve you well.

Setting goals

Once you have an idea of what you want to achieve in the areas outlined previously, you need to think about specific goals. Being specific, you still need to be open-minded, though. There are at least a hundred ways to do most things. So long as you have a general idea of where you're going, you're likely to get there.

Be SMART

A classic technique for goal-setting and management is SMART. It's used by many of the world's top organisations to assess the nature of people's goals. According to SMART, your goals should be:

▨ **S**pecific – Have you clearly defined your goal?

▨ **M**easurable – How do you know if you are making progress?

▨ **A**chievable – Is your goal really achievable? Be ambitious but honest.

▨ **R**ewarding – Is your goal something you are willing to make sacrifices for?

▨ **T**imely – Is your goal achievable in a meaningful timeframe?

Planning your goals

How do you start to achieve your lifetime goals? Once you have set your lifetime goals, life coaching experts recommend setting a twenty-five year plan of smaller goals that you should complete if you are to reach your lifetime plan. Once you have a twenty-five year plan, you should set a five-year plan, a one-year plan, a six-month plan, and a one-month plan. Establish progressively smaller goals that you need to achieve to meet your lifetime goals. Each set of goals should be based on the previous plan.

Set a daily to-do list of things that you should do to work towards your lifetime goals.

The steps you take during the first days and the first months may be very simple. The goals may be to read certain books and otherwise gather information that will help achievement of your goals.

In the beginning you should work to improve the quality and realism of your goal-setting. To stay on track, you should regularly review your plans, and make sure that they continue to fit the way you want to live your life.

When you've decided your first set of plans, establish a habit to review and update your to-do list on a daily basis. Review your longer term plans periodically and modify them to reflect your changing priorities and experiences.

Setting your goals

When it comes to setting your goals, keep this process in mind:

- Write out each goal as a positive statement.

- Be precise when you write your goals and put down dates, times and amounts so that you can measure your achievement.

- Set priorities so that each of your goals has a priority, because this helps you to avoid feeling overwhelmed by too many goals, and helps to direct your attention to the most important ones.

- Write goals down regularly as this helps you keep them focused.

- Keep low-level goals you work to on a daily basis small and achievable, as keeping goals small and incremental gives you more opportunities to reward yourself.

- Take care to set goals over which you have as much control as possible; if you keep your goals focused on personal performance, then you can keep control over the achievement of your goals and draw satisfaction from them.

- It is important to set goals that you can achieve, in full recognition of your own desires and ambitions.

- Do not set goals too low; the best goals are just slightly out of your immediate grasp, but not so far that there is no hope of achieving them.

'As you achieve your goals, short term and long term, be sure to enjoy the satisfaction of having done so.'

As you achieve your goals, short term and long term, be sure to enjoy the satisfaction of having done so. Absorb the implications of the goal achievement. Monitor and revel in your progress towards your life goals. Reward yourself. As you start to make money, make sure you're having fun on the road to millions!

Reviewing your goals

Another important step is to keep reviewing your goals. Check the following:

- Are your goals too easy to achieve? If so, make your next goals harder.

- Are your goals taking too long to achieve? If so, make your next set of goals a little easier to achieve.

- Have you learned something that might lead you to change other goals? If the answer is yes, change the relevant goals.

- Have you noticed a deficit in your skills? If so, set goals to resolve this.

Summing Up

▪ Having your parents actively supporting you through the A level experience not only reinforces your relationship but it is a good reminder that they are invested in your future. If nothing else, it serves as a reminder for you to invest in yourself.

▪ Working to achieve balance in your life is important as you prepare for your A level examinations and pursue A level coursework.

▪ If you are happy at school – well adjusted, enjoying the work, appropriately challenged – you have a greater chance of success at A level than someone who is unhappy in their school environment.

▪ If you are having problems at school, for whatever reason, speak to your parents and teachers. See what they can do to help and what they recommend you do. Remember, your attitude towards school is really important to your A level success.

▪ Acknowledge the importance of schoolwork (including homework) early on in your school experience to help yourself become invested in your A level experience.

▪ Picking a couple of extracurricular activities to pursue during the two years you are studying for A level will help you to achieve and maintain the much needed 'balance' we talked about (and will talk about again).

▪ Be realistic when planning and setting goals, and enjoy the satisfaction of achieving them.

Chapter Three

Choosing A Levels

What are the basics for A level selection?

The selection of A levels these days, is at least a two-step process. After all, you no longer sit for three or four A levels having studied your chosen subjects for two years. Instead, you sit for three or four A1 exams, with scores leading to half of your A level grade. Then, usually dropping a subject, you go on to study for another year – new material – in preparation for another lot of exams, the A2s.

When it comes to the selection of subjects, however, you have the final say. The role of parents, teachers and careers advisors is to provide appropriate guidance and, perhaps even more significantly, serve as a sounding board for the various options you may be weighing up.

'When it comes to the selection of subjects, you have the final say.'

What subjects can be studied at A level?

First of all, there are roughly 40 different subjects you could study at A level. The reality is that few, if any, schools offer to teach each and every A level subject. Second of all, with this rather large number of subjects comes, quite a range to choose from. You will find that in most schools you have the option of studying a number of subjects you could have or did study at GCSE, such as English literature or mathematics, right down to a reasonably long list that covers subjects that are brand new to A level students.

You may have seen via the media, that there has been some debate about the 'best' subjects to study at A level.

Because entry into university and also into the job market is so competitive these days, many people – students and their parents – become very concerned with questions like these: what are the best subjects to study if I want to get into university? What are the subjects most likely to impress university admissions? If I want to go to law school or medical school, what subjects do I need to study at A level?

In most cases, there are multiple answers to these questions. Most answers are also determined by opinion, though, since there is little in the way of conclusive facts to suggest that universities prefer one subject over another, even for some specialist degrees.

The simple truth, and something you should focus on, is that the best A level results are always going to come down to numbers. It makes sense for you to pick a subject you enjoy and one that you can do well in. These things – enjoyment and excellence, shall we say – tend to go hand in hand.

'It makes sense for you to pick a subject you enjoy and one that you can do well in.'

Although it is unlikely you will find any school offering all of the 40 individual subjects, it may be worth looking into the choices. If you want to study something new, for instance, and feel that you can meet the challenge, looking into the course offerings at several different schools may be a good idea.

Subject combinations

Another issue, aside from individual subjects, is the combination of subjects you can choose from. Debates have raged about what subject combinations work best.

Should you study a science and a language to have a balance, or should you concentrate on the sciences or the humanities? What subjects work best if you are planning on studying the law or medicine?

Again, there is really no one answer to the question of subject choices and combinations as a whole. There are, however, three general principles that you should think about and perhaps even talk about with your parents and teachers, as you go through the process of selecting A level subjects.

Choosing subjects you will enjoy

This is a first principle for your A level selection – that you choose a subject you will enjoy.

In fact, this might be the golden rule for any sort of decision-making along these lines. Hopefully you followed this principle to some degree when you made your GCSE selections.

If you enjoy a subject, as we have said, you are more likely to do well in it. Trying to learn something – a subject – that you do not enjoy is quite often a demoralising experience, one that leaves you struggling to make a good grade.

Whatever your career goals, it is important to realise it may well be better for you to take an A level subject you enjoy, that you can do well in, rather than try to pick a subject that you feel you ought to take, for whatever reason.

It is important, though, that you also make an informed decision based on an understanding of what the A level course will involve.

Think about not only the skills required by a given subject but the programme of study for the A level. Talk to your parents or teachers about the course of study in particular and make sure that the topics you will have to study are going to be of interest.

Remember that with subjects such as history, geography, English literature, and so on, the content of the course is going to be different from what you are used to, even after studying the same subject at GCSE.

The skills required may also be different from GCSE to A level, so make sure that your interest in a given subject is likely to hold up at A level as you look to apply this first principle.

If you are thinking about trying a new subject all together because it sounds interesting or because you have an interest in the subject developed outside of school, again, it is important to find out more about the way the subject is taught at A level and how it is assessed. Just because you want to study something like psychology, law or politics, doesn't mean that you are going to necessarily find the subject interesting as it is taught at A level.

Make sure, if you decide to pick a new subject to study at A level, that you understand what the course content is and how the subject is taught. Look also at how the subject is examined. This way, you can make sure that the first principle is actually being followed and you are picking a subject you really are going to enjoy.

Choosing subjects that fit your career plan

This is the second principle: that you should choose subjects which will fit in with your career plans.

'Make sure, if you decide to pick a new subject to study at A level, that you understand what the course content is and how the subject is taught. Look also at how the subject is examined.'

Although we have already discussed the extent to which future career plans should not tie your hands in A level course selection, it is important, particularly if you have a clear career path, to be aware of any subject requirements for university study of a given subject.

There are many degree courses that require certain subjects for entry.

Talk to your school's careers advisor about your career plans and make a list of possible degree subjects. With this list, go to the UCAS website and check for any degree requirements.

Your school should also be able to offer some career advice and even certain forms of testing to help you clarify your long-term plans if you are unsure about what you want to do. It may be a good idea to do this before you finalise A level subjects, although you shouldn't feel you have to finalise any plans at this point.

In fact, consistent with our second principle here, you need to understand that it is generally – almost always, in fact – a bad idea to take a subject you don't enjoy (or don't think you will enjoy) just because it is needed for a particular career.

The only exception is when you have good reason to believe that the subject is going to be easier at A level based on a review of the course details for A level and feedback from teachers.

Discuss subject options with people who know you

This might seem like odd advice but it is all part of taking the time to find out as much as you can about your A level subject options and what will end up being the best choice for you.

To make the right choices, you should not only discuss the first two principles with people you trust but seek out advice from third parties who can offer you an objective and informed opinion on your options.

Talk to your school's careers advisor and your teachers about specific subjects that you are interested in or that you think you might enjoy studying at A level.

Take time to find out all you need to really recognise your own interests, skills, performance levels, and preferred direction after A levels.

Know where you want to go but be prepared to listen to other people, accepting that other people might have good advice and opinions worth considering alongside your own.

At the end of the day, you must make the final decision because you are the one who will be doing the work and living with these choices.

'You must make the final decision because you are the one who will be doing the work and living with these choices.'

Sources of information on A level subjects

To start collecting information about A level subjects and options, look to the following resources:

A level subject guides

There are numerous subject guides for A level. Often these are a good starting point as you are trying to get a handle on the subjects you are considering for A level. Obviously, some guidebooks are better than others but you should be looking for guides that specifically give an outline of content and skills needed and information on how a given subject is assessed.

The best guides will also go into detail on things like subject combination restrictions.

It is likely you will find many of these sorts of books in the general library of your school.

Another option, if you are interested in reviewing these books, is to visit your local library, which might have a wider range of books to review.

Some websites provide online student subject guides, too. If it proves difficult to find relevant books or if you are finding some of the information outdated or limited, turning to the Internet may be a good idea.

Teachers past and present

Beyond books, good sources of information on appropriate subjects are your current, and even past, teachers.

Any competent teacher who has worked with you should have a good knowledge of your intellectual strengths and weaknesses, not to mention a sense of your general skills and knowledge foundation.

As you are working out which subjects you want to study, it is certainly a good idea to ask your teachers – current teachers and any past teachers you particularly trust – about what subjects they think might be a good fit.

Having past and current teachers review A level selections is also a good idea to help confirm that you are making the right choice based on your abilities.

Sixth form teachers

In some instances, the teachers who manage A level subjects are different from those who teach the years leading up to A level, including GCSE. If you are moving to a college to pursue your A levels, then you will also find yourself introduced to a new staff of teachers and thus an additional resource for working out your A level subject selection.

Wherever you plan to complete your A levels, find out which teachers teach the subjects you are considering. See if you can meet with these teachers (perhaps with your parents) to discuss the nature of each subject.

Even though you have not been taught by the sixth form teachers, so they cannot offer an opinion about which subject is right for you, a meeting can still give you an opportunity to ask questions you might have about the A level courses.

Specifications for AS and A2

Yet another excellent resource for you are the AS and A2 specifications, sometimes called exam board syllabuses.

These documents are published by each exam board for the AS and A2 subjects and they describe the topics to be covered for each course.

Note that these documents are also a good resource for your revision because they are often very detailed in their description of the knowledge and skills you are supposed to demonstrate at exam time.

There are three main exam boards that you need to be aware of:

* AQA
* Edexcel
* OCR

You may recognise these boards from your GCSE experience.

Before you go looking for the specifications for the subjects that interest you, though, you will need to determine which exam board is used by your school for each subject you are considering.

You can find exam board syllabuses for both AS and A2 requirements for each A level subject online at the three main exam board websites.

Other students

Just as you may want to speak to other sixth-formers or those who have recently finished their A level courses about the A level experience, consider talking to these same types of people about subject choices.

Talk to sixth-formers who are currently studying the subjects you are considering.

'You can find exam board syllabuses for both AS and A2 requirements for each A level subject online at the three main exam board websites.'

Questions to ask include:

- What do you like best about the subject in general?
- What do you like best about the AS/A2 course?
- What do you dislike about the course?
- What have you found to be (the most) challenging?

Texts and reference books

As you are reviewing syllabuses for courses your are interested in and also taking to people who have studied certain subjects at A level, another option is also to review the textbooks and reference books used for your shortlisted subjects.

Skimming through these books is another way to give yourself a sense of the type of work that you will be doing if you opt for any given course.

Reviewing textbooks and reference books can also be particularly useful when you are considering choosing a subject that you have never studied before, as these sources can give a sense of how the subject is going to be taught.

Considering A level requirements for degrees

As we have said already, there are few hard and fast rules about A level requirements for specific degrees. In most cases, if you have good grades and some general evidence of your interest in a given subject, you have as good a shot as anyone to be accepted for any undergraduate major of their choice.

Say you want to study law. You should have a good shot at getting a place on the course of your choice if you have good grades at A level and if, for instance, you can demonstrate your interest in law by having a list of extracurricular activities that complement your interests.

While there are few rules, however, there are some general guidelines for certain subjects, particularly those leading to demanding careers.

Chemistry, for instance, is usually a subject recommended at A level for anyone considering a career in medicine, veterinary sciences, dentistry, pharmaceuticals, or biology. Biology would also be a good choice for anyone considering these kinds of careers.

For a degree in law, it is useful (but again, not required) to have a range of subjects demonstrating cognitive ability and the ability to write. An A level in law is not usually recommended and is certainly not required.

For a degree in business studies, it is usually a good idea to have a focus on subjects such as mathematics or economics. A levels in business studies or economics can be helpful leading towards a career in accounting, too.

Anyone considering a course in European Business Studies or similar is strongly recommended to pursue an A level in a European language (French, German or Spanish, primarily).

Prospective psychology majors also do well to have a mix of arts/humanities subjects and the science.

For computing and engineering, A level mathematics is usually strongly recommended. A few universities require it, at least for computing. Maths and physics are generally recommended for engineering while chemical engineering courses strongly recommend chemistry (as you would expect).

As a general rule:

- Most degree courses expect you to study at least one subject that is strongly demonstrative of your interest in the degree course (e.g. study history at A level if you want to study it at university).

- Top academic degree courses usually require three solid academic A levels (so no courses like psychology, business studies, law at A level).

How many subjects should you take?

One question many parents and many A level students have is how many subjects a student should take at A level.

'Most degree courses expect you to study at least one subject that is strongly demonstrative of your interest in the degree course.'

Most people take four subjects at AS and discountinue one of these subjects at A2. However, not everyone is able to manage the demands of this many courses. Other people are actually able to study an additional A level without issue.

Unless your teachers or advisor recommends that you pursue fewer or more than four AS levels and fewer or more than three A2 levels, it is likely that subject number – number of A levels – is not even going to be an issue.

However, if you know you were struggling academically at GCSE, as you are advancing to A level, or if you have reason to believe that your academic performance is well above average level, then you may want to ask about the possibility for adjusting the subject numbers to better reflect your needs and abilities.

Which subjects should you drop at A2?

You do have to make a decision about which subject to drop from AS to A2. Although there are no definite rules about which subject you should drop when it comes time to transition from AS to A2, there are a few factors to consider:

- AS scores.
- Interest levels in the subjects.
- Skills and knowledge of the subjects.
- Career goals.

Considering some or all of these elements will help you make a smart decision about the AS to A2 transition.

Summing Up

- A level subject selection is a serious thing – you have to live with your choices beyond the two years of the A level course.

- A level choices and results affect educational and career options.

- It is most important to pick an A level subject you are going to enjoy.

- Reviewing A level options ahead of time is important for ensuring that you make the right decision.

- Consulting multiple sources of information (teachers, past students, textbooks, books, syllabuses, etc.) is helpful to giving a sense of what each subject choice involves.

- There are no hard or fast rules about what subject you need to study for a given degree but always make sure that you check your A level subject choices against entry requirements for prospective universities before making a final selection.

Chapter Four

Balancing Time and Building Skill Sets Through Years 12 and 13

Defining time management for A level students

So what is 'time management'?

Quite simply, it is the application of certain principles or systems to organise and use time effectively. Often, it goes hand in hand with goal management designed to help a person prioritise what they need to work on at any given time.

Since everyone is different, time management and goal management system selection often involves trial and error to find out which approach will work best.

Creating and sticking to a schedule

Not only does everyone work in different ways, every teenager has different demands placed upon them these days.

Their schedules are going to be determined by school demands, extracurricular demands, family demands and social demands.

The first step to identifying the minute-to-minute details, however, is to write a list of things you do on a daily basis, e.g. wake up, take a shower, go to school, do homework, do chores, etc.

The second step is to write a list of the things you needs to do on a weekly basis. This list might include things like extracurricular activities, sports activities and social activities.

A third list might include monthly activities and other special events.

With these three lists drawn up, it will help you identify a single calendar system. The system could be online, set up somewhere like Google Calendars. In fact, this is a good idea because you can set reminders and alarms for events, as well as create to-do lists.

If you work better when you write things down, a planner would probably be best.

The most important point is that there be a single system and that it be used consistently.

'Tracking time, however, is really the first step to effective time management for anyone, including students.'

Tips for managing time

With a schedule and calendar in place, there are a few strategies you can try to maximise the effectiveness of the more basic time management system:

Track time

These days, it is very easy to set timers and keep a record of how your time is spent. It is easy enough to do on a computer or a mobile phone.

Tracking time, however, is really the first step to effective time management for anyone, including students.

Recording what you are doing, when, and for how long, you get a sense of several things. First, you get a sense of how well you are managing your time. Second, you can also get a sense of whether you are effectively prioritising your time. Third, you can also check for and eliminate activities that are a waste of time.

Take regular breaks

To reduce stress and increase focus long term, it is a good idea to take regular breaks from revision (set reminders to take breaks if you are prone to forgetting).

Breaks should occur both between sessions and at various times, staggered throughout the day. Breaks might be up to about 15 minutes at a time.

Effective breaks might involve focused breathing for several minutes at a time, even meditation.

If you are the type of person who enjoys being outside, being able to walk about to clear their head, take advantage of this and incorporate some outdoor time into your break times.

If you enjoy meditating or even just closing your eyes for a few minutes, or power napping to replenish yourself, don't be afraid to try these techniques out in your revision work.

Create homework time at school

Because it limits distractions, it is often a good idea for students to complete homework tasks at school rather than at home. Homework time at school could be during lunch or during break time.

Many A level students have free or study periods. These are also ideal for homework time at school. And the more homework you manage to complete at school, the more time you will have in the evening to fit in other activities, revision activities, and relaxation time.

Prioritisation as a time management tool

Goal-setting fits in with time management as a system for organising what you need to get done each day, each week, each month. For A levels, however, goal-setting or prioritisation of tasks, will help you manage your course load effectively.

'To reduce stress and increase focus long term, it is a good idea to take regular breaks from revision (set reminders to take breaks if you are prone to forgetting).'

Simple prioritisation strategies

The simplest and perhaps the easiest way to prioritise tasks is using a system for urgent, normal and low priority.

If you make a list of your tasks for each period of time – every day, for instance – you can also get into the habit of marking tasks according to this priority scale.

Urgent tasks are those that require immediate attention or that are very important, for instance, coursework pieces.

Normal priority tasks are those that need to be completed but are less urgent or less important than, for instance, coursework or specific exam revision.

Low priority tasks are those that can perhaps be put off for a day or so.

'Goal-setting or prioritisation of tasks, will help you manage your course load effectively.'

When it comes to dividing up your time, you can then refer to your tasks according to priority.

Setting aside the tasks that cannot be avoided, such as going to school, travelling to and from school, eating meals, etc., you can work out how much time you have free to focus on different types of projects.

Tasks can then be divided up in the remaining available slots.

The 'top three tasks' approach for the overwhemed student

If, for whatever reason, you begin to feel really overwhelmed by the list of things you have to do as you are preparing for A level – and most A level students have a long list to work through – a good task management system might be the 'top three' approach. Instead of worrying about everything you need to try and do, write a daily list of the top three things you must do from your general task list.

Concentrating on only these three things within the time you have available, will help if you are feeling overwhelmed and enable you to get a good handle on your work.

Setting a timer may also help to improve focus.

Most teenagers and adults can focus for about 45 minutes on a single task. Working on the top three tasks, work for intervals of 45 minutes, followed by a 5 to 15-minute break to complete homework or even chores.

Not only will this approach help you to manage your to-do list daily, it will also help instil good habits, preparing you to be that much more effective at university and beyond.

The 'getting it done' approach to stay motivated

If you really want to develop positive goal and task management, teaching yourself to use a system like 'getting it done' might be something to consider.

Online, you can find a whole range of resources related to this particular style of goal and task management.

If you struggle to stay motivated to keep up with this kind of systematic planning, it might also be a good choice to use this system because it really can be a fun exercise.

Summing Up

- Learning to manage time effectively is crucial for A level success.

- Skills related to time management and prioritisation of goals are really important for success at A level, so make sure you are supported when it comes to implementing theses skills.

- Consider investing in time management and goal management programmes for yourself; there are a whole range of apps and software programmes that support goal managment, Google offers some useful programmes online.

- The more you can do to consistently manage your time and set goals for work and your personal life, the better you are preparing not only for A level success but also for success at university and in the workplace.

Chapter Five

Making the Most of Module Exams and Coursework

What are module exams?

You have exams (AS exams) in the summer of your first year of sixth form (Year 12). Depending on what subjects you are studying, you may also have what are called module exams in January of Year 12 or Year 13.

Retakes are usually done in January, too.

A levels are normally made up of either four or six separate units. What you learn in each of these units has to be tested. Module exams are simply a way of testing your understanding of what you have learned in each of these units.

Usually, you have to complete two or three units in your first year of A level study, in preparation for your main AS level examinations over the summer. In some cases, you can opt to take certain module exams earlier in the year, in January. Modules can also be retaken, and retakes are usually done in January, too.

Module exams are common for certain subjects like mathematics, the sciences, and some humanities subjects.

'Module exams are common for certain subjects like mathematics, the sciences, and some humanities subjects.'

What is coursework?

Some 'modules' at A level are graded, not based on exam results but based on coursework produced by your child.

Coursework could be anything from a lengthy written piece, an experiment, a piece of artwork or a design project.

Whether you have coursework will depend on your course of study – both the subject and the exam board.

In some instances, you may even have a choice as to whether you complete a module by submitting coursework or by taking another exam.

'With coursework, a broader range of skills may be tested, including skills related to project planning and creativity, not to mention time management and goal setting.'

What are the pros and cons of coursework modules?

The advantage of choosing coursework modules, obviously, is that you have one less exam to deal with. Many teachers recognise the advantage of this and so you may find that several of your A level grades are based on coursework modules.

The disadvantage of coursework, though, is that it can be extremely time-consuming. The stress of undertaking coursework in addition to the regular workload applied at A level may be detrimental. Another factor can be the nature of coursework itself, that it tests skills that may be different from those tested in an exam scenario. Whereas you are likely to revise facts and practise specific ways of answering questions in preparation for examination under test conditions, with coursework, a broader range of skills may be tested, including skills related to project planning and creativity, not to mention time management and goal setting – some skills we have mentioned earlier as being important for A level success.

Preparing for and monitoring performance across modules

Regardless of whether you do better in exam settings or when working more independently and across a longer period of time, what you need to be most aware of with modules is that they are scored and the scores for each module go towards your final grade.

Assess how well you are going to perform in each module. That is, consider whether it is a module covering topics and testing skills that a) you are interested in and b) you are able to learn and recall easily.

Not every module of your course is likely to be as easy as the others. You, as an individual learner, may struggle with one module, one area of A level study, and no other, simply because of individual needs.

Try to keep a clear picture of when and where you are likely to struggle in a typical exam or in a coursework scenario. Not only that, but you can also apply this information to have support in place as you are working on topics or skills that you find more challenging to work on than others.

Monitoring your performance in each module has another benefit, though. At AS level, you will be in a position to assess how well you have done in given modules of coursework or testing, probably both. When you have AS or indeed any other A level results in hand, you can start to make determinations about whether you should consider retaking a particular module to improve your score.

Another issue that can more effectively be addressed with module scores is what score you need to achieve across other modules to earn a particular grade in your chosen A level course.

This information – module scores – can help you plan and manage your time.

Summing Up

- You will study either four or six modules for A level – two or three modules will be studied per year over the two-year period.

- Each module will be assessed, either under test conditions or on the basis of coursework.

- In most cases, you will not have the option to choose how each module is tested (whether you take an exam or produce coursework). However, if you are given a choice, it is important that you consider your overall strengths in testing scenarios – whether you tend to perform better under exam conditions or with more time and resources to exercise creativity.

- Reviewing module scores as they are available to you will help in the transition from AS to A2 and in the prioritisation of goals and management of time.

Chapter Six

Managing Study Leave

What is study leave?

Prior to A level examinations, most students are given the option to take 'study leave'.

Study leave is a break from school. It is an opportunity to work at home or anywhere else you choose that is not school.

Why is it important?

One of the goals of the A level experience is to help students learn to be more independent and to have them take more personal accountability in their learning and in their work.

Study leave usually begins a couple of weeks before exams begin. This means there is a good portion of time for you to set up a study schedule and really get some focused revision done.

Provided you are sensible with this time (i.e. not using study leave as holiday time) then the major benefit of study leave is that it allows you to cut out a lot of time-wasting activity.

Time-wasting activity isn't just about sitting around on the couch, playing video games, or talking on the phone. Daily activities like travel to and from school can be unduly time wasting too.

'Study leave is a break from school. It is an opportunity to work at home or anywhere else you choose that is not school.'

What can you do to use study leave effectively?

Everyone learns differently and everyone studies differently. Give yourself some space to discover or rediscover what studying style works best for you, especially when it comes to study leave.

Generally speaking, the secret to managing study leave effectively is to plan it – to know what time there is available to study and to figure out how to use that time effectively.

The best way to manage study leave is with planning and scheduling tools that are designed to manage your time effectively – a calendar/schedule and a timer.

As we've already suggested, learning to manage your time with schedules and calendars will help you to learn time management skills and goal-setting for the purpose of prioritisation. When you master these skills, you will be in a position to manage study leave effectively.

However, when it comes to study leave, keep in mind some general advice about managing stress and balancing time.

If you find yourself spending your study leave buried in books, working flat out with no breaks and no time to relax, you should rethink your approach.

Overworking the body and brain is as problematic for exam success as under-working it.

Remember that the most successful students, without exception, are the ones who develop structured, productive, balanced routines for their schoolwork and revision. They give themselves enough time to sleep properly, time to get some exercise, time to relax and have fun, and time to work.

'The most successful students, without exception, are the ones who develop structured, productive, balanced routines for their schoolwork and revision.'

Time management suggestions

Although everyone works differently, early morning and early afternoon are good times to undertake more intensive revision and work. The afternoon and early evening times are generally better for less intense revision, such as background reading. However, if you decide to undertake less demanding revision work at this time, you may want to think about having a coffee on hand because this is also a time of day in which people become quite drowsy. You should consider not only a coffee, in fact, but a carbohydrates boost – a banana or another healthy carbohydrates snack to jolt your energy and overall alertness.

What strategies are particularly effective for studying during this break?

Once you have an effective schedule in place and workable goals, the last thing you can really do to ensure that you are using study leave effectively is to make sure that your study approach is an efficient one.

Reviewing syllabuses and learned materials

Before you start revising, it is important that you go through the list of topics pertaining to your course of study, reviewing the elements that need to be covered based on the syllabus.

First, nobody can revise what they have not learned in the first place.

The first thing you need to check is that you have actually learned everything that is going to be, or could be, covered in the exam.

Ideally, you should have at least one copy of your course syllabus to look at before you start your revision in earnest. Most of these documents are available online in their latest edition so print off a couple of copies if you need to and go through them, highlighting any areas in the syllabus that you feel you have not yet covered in class.

Another thing you can do, once you have identified any actual gaps in your learning, is go through a copy of the syllabus with a couple of different coloured highlighters. To keep things simple, try using three different highlighters – a red or pink highlighter, an orange highlighter and a green highlighter.

Designate each colour with a specific value:

- Red can indicate a topic or a key point – an element of the syllabus – that

'Nobody can revise what they have not learned in the first place.'

you feel you are going to have to incorporate as a priority in your revision. For instance, if you feel that you really do not have a solid grasp of a specific concept that is a component of your syllabus, highlight references to the concept in red, indicating that this is material that you need to concentrate on in your revision.

- Orange can indicate topics or key points that you are relatively familiar with but feel that you still need to work on quite a bit.

- You can use a green highlighter for topics or key concepts that you are particularly comfortable with.

Organise learning materials

'It is important that all the relevant class notes and learning materials are collected and organised before revision starts.'

Once you have highlighted specific topics and prioritised them with colour-coding, you need to create some kind of database for organising the topics you need to cover in your revision and the learning materials you have to work with in order to cover them all.

Make a list of topics and keywords from the syllabus of each subject you are working on.

Then list learning materials by categories.

In most instances, you are going to have books and articles to work with, as well as textbooks, class notes, handbooks from teachers, and other resources.

For each topic and keyword, make a list of the learning materials that are going to be relevant.

It is important that all the relevant class notes and learning materials are collected and organised before revision starts. Any books you need to look for should be on hand.

To organise your learning material effectively, try creating a database working from the revision topics you have outlined.

Prioritise learning topics

Ideally, you should also have access to past papers or exam questions for the last two to three years. The reason for this will allow you to see which topics covered on the syllabuses that have already come up.

At the very least, knowing what has already been covered will help you to prioritise topics for revision.

Identify the most productive time of day

Think about what time of day you work most effectively. Some people work best early in the morning. Others work best late at night. Some are more alert and more effective during the afternoon.

Since you have already been through exams (GCSEs) you should have a pretty good idea when you can revise best – when you are going to be best able to actually memorise key information and when you are going to be able to focus on, for instance, working through practice exam questions.

Using this information, you should apply the specific times of day for revision, breaking up the time into small periods – between forty minutes to an hour.

The time period that works best for you is going to be determined by your concentration span – and everyone's concentration span varies.

If you are easily distracted, then keep your revision sessions short – about forty minutes – taking short breaks between those periods so that your concentration does not suffer.

If you have a good concentration span, working for up to an hour on a given subject may be fine. It can also be appropriate for you to block off a couple of hours of back-to-back study, avoiding any possible overloading of the concentration span, and then following up with a short break, although longer breaks can be allowed.

'If you are easily distracted, then keep your revision sessions short.'

Identifying the most effective revision techniques

As we've said, everyone studies differently. Different revision techniques are going to work for you versus everyone else.

Some techniques you can try if you are struggling to figure out what to do are:

- Note taking – This is by far the most common form of revision but it is generally not enough, by itself, to constitute effective revision for A level exams. Using note taking as a revision strategy, you should be focusing on reviewing course materials – class notes, textbooks, etc. – and rewriting the information to constitute notes that are easy to memorise. One way to maximise the effectiveness of note taking, though, is to catalogue information in several different ways. Keywords and concepts should be highlighted and organised throughout the note system to create multiple associations and links between key ideas. This system for organisation is somewhat similar to the system used to organise topics and keywords from your syllabuses.

- Revision cards – Although these are very similar to notes generated in the note taking strategy we just talked about, the key difference between notes and revision cards is that the cards are a much more condensed. They are particularly good for memorisation because of this.

- Diagrams and charts – Visual learners benefit most from the use of diagrams and charts, at least when it comes to memorisation of facts, ideas and key concepts. The effectiveness of diagrams and charts, however, can be maximised through the use of multiple colour systems, keyword and concept systems, and systems for organised development of these charts and diagrams. Creating diagrams and charts and posting them on walls or other surfaces can be very useful for visual learners. For planning/organising essay responses, diagrams and charts can be very helpful too. So if you do (or think you might) work effectively with this kind of support, knowing that you are going to have some written responses to produce in your exams, practise using diagrams and charts to outline such responses.

- Group or paired revision – Sometimes two heads are better than one. Sometimes people learn better when they have one or more people learning and revising with them. So long as the focus is actually on revision – not socialising or otherwise wasting time – if you want to revise with a study

'Visual learners benefit most from the use of diagrams and charts, at least when it comes to memorisation of facts, ideas and key concepts.'

group or you think that you might revise more effectively with a partner or group of partners, consider using this revision approach. A key advantage, is that students can test each other on exam topics and issues. They can also provide constructive criticism and feedback on how well one person is understanding and remembering concepts and facts, not to mention how well they are answering questions that are asked of them. If you are taking one or more foreign language at A level, group learning may also be a great idea for preparing for oral and listening exams.

Summing Up

- Learning to manage study leave effectively is an important part of preparing, not only for your A level exams but also for higher education and eventually a career.

- It is also important for relaxation and revision prior to exam day.

- Since you have most likely experienced 'study leave' before, you should be relatively familiar with what it entails.

- The key to making study leave successful is time management.

- Study leave is not a break from work or an opportunity to do other things (work, hang out with friends, do nothing etc.).

- Responsible work and revision habits are important and you should make them a priority both prior to and during study leave.

- You need to find a revision strategy that works for you, keeping in mind that everyone learns differently and different subjects may be better studied in a particular way (e.g. foreign language study might benefit from group study).

Chapter Seven

Before Exam Day

Establishing exam day schedules

Assuming you revise and manage your time relatively well (incorporating some of the ideas we have suggested), at some point during AS and A2, you are going to need to begin preparing for actual exams.

For several reasons, though, you need an exam day schedule. Not only do you need to make sure that the date, time and location of exams are effectively written down, it helps to have a schedule in place on exam day to minimise stress and help ensure that you get to your exam location on time.

Make sure you write down the time, date, and location of exams and post the information in several different places – prominently.

It is not uncommon for students (and parents) to misread this crucial information about exams (and other important appointments), especially if the information is being checked at the last minute.

Save yourself the stress of missing your exams or going to the wrong location by establishing a couple of reminders both prior to and on the day of the exam.

Organising yourself for exam day

Preparation is the father of inspiration, so make sure that you do all you can to prepare yourself for exam success.

'Make sure you write down the time, date, and location of exams and post the information in several different places – prominently.'

Getting the right equipment

The day before your first exam, at the very latest, make sure that you have the following ready to take with you to your exam, a kind of 'exam kit':

- 2B pencils.
- At least three blue or black ink biros, or reliable roller ball pens or ink cartridge pens.
- If you have ink or roller ball pens, have back-up pens (at least two) and back-up refills for the ink.
- Two erasers.
- A ruler.
- Any special equipment, e.g. maths, science and general studies exams may require a calculator, a compass; certain exams may also require you to take texts (books) that you have been studying.

'It is important that you get a good amount of sleep prior to exam day.'

To keep this equipment together, take either a plastic bag, a couple of elastic bands, or a clear pencil case.

Clothing and shoes also constitute equipment for exams – you should be wearing comfortable clothes and shoes.

Layers may be a good idea, as exam rooms can sometimes be very cold or very warm and the weather outside may be totally different.

Getting a good night's sleep

- It is going to be important that you are able to focus for a considerable length of time on exam day. To give yourself the best chance of managing this, it is important that you get a good amount of sleep prior to exam day.
- Avoiding late night revision is important.
- Avoiding television time or staying out late is also important.
- For the body to feel rested, it must have the opportunity to go through a normal sleep cycle – that means as little interruption as possible.
- Make sure that you go to bed and to sleep early on the nights before exams.

60

- Ideally, you should get somewhere between 7 and 9 hours of sleep on the nights before your exams.

It may also be a good idea to set your alarm about half an hour to an hour before you usually get up so that you are giving yourself a head start. This way, you will have more time to wake up on exam day, to take a shower and eat a proper breakfast. Having time to go through these routines will help you stay calm. The more you have to rush, the more aware you become of what you have in front of you. The more aware you are, the more likely you are to start feeling overwhelmed or panicked. It might even be that you simply end up thinking about what you have been revising in preparation for your exam. Even this is not the best idea on the morning before an exam. You should try to be clear-headed, calm and relaxed. Your focus will kick in when you are sitting down at your desk, not before.

Minimising the need to rush out the door also helps to minimise exam stress and maximise efficiency on the day.

Make sure you are eating properly

There's a lot of information out there about the benefits of a balanced diet for the maintenance of concentration and energy levels. For A level success, it is important that you are eating properly, especially on exam day.

On exam day, like every other day, the most important meal is definitely breakfast. This is the meal that jump-starts your body, boosting your energy levels but boosting them appropriately, so long as you make healthy choices about food.

One of the reasons you should set your alarm half an hour early, is so you can take the time to enjoy a hearty breakfast.

Protein is the essential element for an exam-day breakfast. The benefit of protein is that it provides a fairly steady release of energy.

A breakfast of eggs, cheese, or other high-protein foods is a good idea versus high-sugar cereals. The disadvantage of high-sugar foods, especially for breakfast, is that they provide a sudden burst of energy followed by an inevitable crash.

Having a steady energy level is going to be important.

In addition to a high-protein breakfast, though, it does make sense to have snacks available. But rather than chocolate bars or junk food, get yourself a supply of healthy snack fruits, like bananas, apples, granola bars, etc.

A supply of bottled water is also a good idea on exam day.

Helping yourself to slow down

One of the big reasons to get up early and make sure you know where you are going, is that you need to avoid going anywhere in too much of a hurry.

As we have suggested already, if you are rushing about in the early morning before your exam, it is going to be difficult to refocus on your exam once you are sitting down and are being told to get started on your work. Everyone needs some time for transition, but it is your responsibility to make sure you get it on exam day. You have to give yourself that time by being methodical and organised.

Another problem with rushing is that it tends to leave you less than level-headed. It is not unknown for there to be issues with getting from A to B, especially when you are in a rush.

If you are in a rush and finding that things are not absolutely going your way on exam day, even before you have sat down to your examination, you are likely to have issues with even the most practical of steps, such as finding an alternate route to get to school on time if there happens to be an issue.

Make sure you breathe – take a series of deep breaths – if you are feeling overwhelmed on exam day. Some people find that walking or pacing helps to calm their nerves, others find that stretching is a good relaxation technique. Find out what works for you.

Prior to exam day, it is going to be helpful to identify one or two techniques for slowing down and calming down if you are beginning to feel overwhelmed.

Last-minute revision

Don't overload on the last-minute revision – emphasise this to yourself as a final pointer for preparing for exams.

In theory, it should only be necessary for you to do a final check of key facts and pointers if you have actually done your revision. You may not feel that you have done as much revision as you could have. You may be panicking thinking that you haven't covered everything. Chances are, though, that you are not the most objective person when it comes to assessing this issue. In fact, hours, minutes before your exam, you are very likely going to experience self-doubt and worry about what you have been studying – have you done a good job remembering everything you need to?

In all likelihood, you will think 'no', but tell yourself 'yes'.

Don't let negative feelings cloud your judgement at the last minute.

Even if you have not managed to effectively prepare for your exams, it is only going to increase your stress levels to try and learn new information when you have just hours or even minutes to spare. It will amount to an ineffective use of time. It is far better, if you are unprepared, to focus on remaining calm and focused; keeping things in perspective.

'Don't overload on the last-minute revision.'

If you are really not prepared for your exams, try to avoid being too critical with yourself. Let yourself go through the experience and remind yourself that if you come out without the results you wanted, you can always try another angle.

Summing Up

▪ Your main goal on exam day is to work to minimise your stress levels.

▪ Make sure you know the time, date, and location of the exam; double-check this information for accuracy before exam day but also check on exam day.

▪ Eat a healthy breakfast and pack a collection of healthy snacks plus water to keep energy up during exams.

▪ Use a couple of relaxation techniques to help yourself focus and stay calm right before your exam experience begins.

▪ Minimise last-minute disasters by having back-up plans in place if, for instance, you miss a bus or leave your pens and pencils at home. Be prepared for exam day issues in order to avoid them.

▪ It is extremely important that you avoid last-minute revision. Repeat this as a mantra to yourself.

Chapter Eight

Getting Through the Exam Period

Take it one day at a time

Perhaps the hardest thing about the exam period is dealing with the ups and downs of stress levels. You will probably find yourself close to being at your peak for stress and anxiety.

How do you survive?

The simple answer – take it a day at a time.

Give yourself plenty of opportunity to relax and try to keep the lines of communication open with your family as much as possible, to minimise stress and conflict that may be brought on by simple misunderstanding or misjudgement of how you are feeling.

Try to help parents, family and friends understand that you are going through a lot and probably worrying about a lot of things at once. After all, it is very common for A level students to be anxious and stressed out about revision and individual exams, even if they are very well prepared and very capable of performing well.

'Perhaps the hardest thing about the exam period is dealing with the ups and downs of stress levels.'

Work to reduce your stress levels

On the other hand, it is extremely unhelpful if you are getting so anxious that you are spending more time worrying about your exams than actually revising or preparing for exams.

Learning a couple of relaxation techniques and incorporating them into your day may be a good idea.

One technique to simply improve your overall feelings about what you have going on in your life is to change the language you are using.

Avoid saying or thinking things that are negative like:

- I don't understand . . .
- I'm frustrated that . . .
- I hate my . . .
- I can't figure out . . .
- I'm stressed about . . .
- I'm worried that . . .
- I should be able to . . . but I can't . . .
- Why am I having so much trouble?

Sometimes by making even this small change to your mindset, you can start to feel much better about what you have in front of you.

A basic meditation technique to try out to help you relax and focus involves simply concentrating on your breath. You should also try to visualise letting go of your thoughts as much as possible, but don't try too hard to push them if they don't want to move out of your mind.

Step by step, a simple meditation technique you can employ anywhere is as follows:

- Sit or lie down, making sure you're comfortable.
- Close your eyes.
- Become aware of each part of your body for a moment, and feel the tension leaving it. Start at your toes and work up to your head.
- Shift your focus to your breath.
- Breathe through your nose, deeply at first, but after a couple of deep breaths, breathe in whatever way feels the most comfortable.

- If you start to think about anything, if any thoughts start to creep into your mind, dismiss them and return your attention to your breath.
- Keep on returning your attention to your breath.

When you are done, simply open your eyes and breathe deeply once more.

Talk it through

Help your family to be understanding and supportive during study leave and during your exams. The best way to do this is probably to talk to them – to your parents in particular.

For one thing, evidence shows that simply talking about stressful situations can go a long way to reducing stress but consider setting aside a regular time to talk to your parents them about what you are worrying about.

Give yourself the night off every now and again

Another strategy that may very well go hand in hand with simply talking, is taking some time to relax.

Set aside an evening and take the time to read a book or watch a movie, go for a walk in the park or perhaps go out for a quiet evening.

This strategy works simply because A level students can feel that their work is becoming monotonous or their revision is becoming ineffective, when they are stuck staring at their books and other revision materials for extended periods.

Develop a strategy for test taking

There are a number of strategies for answering questions. Having a workable strategy for yourself, though – one that you have practised as part of your revision – will help you feel more in control as exams approach.

Among the most effective strategies are the following:

'Help your family to be understanding and supportive during study leave and during your exams.'

- **Answering all the questions, even if you don't know the answer** – This is a strategy that works for multiple choice tests; you can also apply this strategy if you think you might have at least a vague idea of what the answer to a question might be.

- **Answering questions with the most marks first** – If you struggle to get through exams to answer all questions, then learning to identify the question with the most available marks and beginning with it may be a good way to maximise the potential for exam success. If you miss out only those questions that have a small number of marks available, you at least make it possible to achieve a high score if you have answered the most valuable questions first.

'Spending too much time on a single question tends to leave you without enough time to answer the remaining questions, costing a lot of marks.'

- **Avoid spending too long on any one question (also known as pacing)** – If you get stuck on a single question or a series of questions in your exam, spending too much time on those quetions in proportion to the number of questions in the exam, the marks available, and the time allowed, you risk a poor grade. Spending too much time on a single question tends to leave you without enough time to answer the remaining questions, costing a lot of marks. Pacing is something you can work on when you undertake practice exams and it is perhaps even something you can work on at home with your parents to support you, having them oversee your efforts as you work through practice exams.

- **Allow time to double-check answers** – Being thorough is often particularly difficult when you are under exam pressure. However, if you can to get into the habit of double-checking, even triple-checking your answers to questions, you are going to help yourself avoid careless mistakes.

- **Tackle difficult questions last** – If you encounter a difficult question and you have other questions remaining, leave it, you can always come back to it later.

Make sure you read (and then re-read) the instructions – This is something that your teachers will most likely repeat several times over. Careless mistakes are going to be one of your biggest nemeses when you are going through A level exams (as they probably were at GCSE, too). Everyone makes mistakes under pressure, when they are anxious. The more you can do to avoid these types of mistakes, the more you can stay relaxed through the exam period.

Beyond these tips and strategies, make reading the question several times something you do every time you sit down to undertake an exam. You should also make a habit of reviewing the front page of your answer booklet and any other sources of exam instructions for clarification on instructions. Double-checking this information will certainly improve your chances of success at A level, again by cutting down on the risk for careless mistakes in how questions are answered.

Forget about each exam once it is over

This is another one of those pieces of advice that just about everyone offers to students facing A level or GCSE exams. Still, if you can actually follow it, you will almost certainly set yourself on the path to success in the end.

A major problem with exam stress is that it can build as the exam period continues. If you can learn to detach yourself from each individual exam once it is complete, you can increase your chances of exam success overall.

Everyone tends to feel different after their exams. Many wish they had more time. Many others openly worry about the answers they gave to specific questions in the exam.

To save yourself a lot of worry, though, try to avoid discussing your answers or any kinds of concerns with your fellow students. After all, there is no advantage. You can't go back in time to check that you remember the details of an answer you gave.

The best thing you can do, once your exams are done, is forget about them and go and do something to help yourself relax, replenish and hit the ground running with the revision you have left do.

When you are finished with all of your exams, you might want to take a day or two to really reward yourself. Once you have gotten through your final A level exam, you have come through the A level experience. Although you have to await results, you can at least congratulate yourself for putting in the effort and sticking with it.

'To save yourself a lot of worry, try to avoid discussing your answers or any kinds of concerns with your fellow students.'

Plan for tomorrow

It is very likely that you will do a lot of planning before your A levels are actually over, but once you have your exams out of the way, even if you have done a lot of the leg work already, you can finally turn your attentions to what lies ahead for you in life.

Perhaps the most obvious thing to look at for planning are your university choices. Once you have finished with AS exams, the summer before you begin your final year of study, you might consider planning tours of universities.

The summer before Year 13 is a really good time for putting in some of the leg work to figure out your university choices. Hopefully by the end of Year 13, you will be ready with your top choices for university and your offers from specific institutions.

With A level exams out of the way, you can think about preparing in earnest for the next phase of your life, which most likely includes a university placement leading to a career in just a few short years.

'When you are finished with all of your exams, take a day or two to really reward yourself.'

As a prospective university student, you are going to be expected to live and work even more independently than you have through your A level studies. While this can seem like a daunting prospect, it is also an exciting one and one that you can be preparing for over the summer, after your A2 exams. At the very least, it is a great way to distract yourself.

Here are a few suggestions for making the most of this period and also keeping your mind off A level results:

Get some work experience

Colleges and employers are always impressed when you can demonstrate your interest in a given subject or career. One of the best ways to do this by the time you are working on or even done with your A levels, is by having a couple of work experience placements under your belt.

Make a list of the careers/jobs you are interested in or just the degree subjects you are considering.

Work out a list of relevant jobs that you might like to 'try out' by way of work experience.

Go to your school careers advisor if you need help figuring out these details.

Once you have a list, check out some local businesses or talk to your careers advisor about prospective work experience placements that they might recommend based on your interests.

See if you can get a job for the summer to get some useful experience and distract yourself.

Earn some money and extend your CV

While most work experience placements are unpaid, you can also get useful work experience (and save up a bit for university) by working as a paid employee.

You may have had a job throughout sixth form (a part-time one), which can be a great and is maybe something to look forward to once your exams are out of the way.

Learn something new

Assuming you are not burnt out by revision, consider taking up a new hobby or even studying a new skill or subject in some way over your summer break.

'Colleges and employers are always impressed when you can demonstrate your interest in a given subject or career.'

Summing Up

▪ Give yourself plenty of opportunity to relax and de-stress as you work through the exam period.

▪ Learn a couple of basic relaxation techniques to help yourself maintain focus and reduce anxiety.

▪ Talk to your friends and family about any problems you are experiencing. Not only will talking help you keep the lines of communication open, it may very well help you cure your anxiety all together.

▪ Motivate yourself to get through the exam period by planning ahead.

Chapter Nine

Success or Failure: How to Cope With Results Day

Keeping things in perspective

Results day tends to creep up on you. Hopefully, though, you have prepared for this day. You should have your target – your ideal outcomes – which were the goals for study, revision, and exam periods. Of course, you have probably been through the university application process and have heard back from most if not all of the institutions on whether or not there is a place available. You should also have a couple of back-up plans that you have discussed with your parents and that you all feel comfortable with.

Sitting down with your careers advisor for a collaborative discussion on options may be a good idea if you feel overwhelmed with this planning process.

Even with a post-A level plan in place, though, results day is going to be intimidating. The best thing you can do to help yourself get through it is stay calm. Decide whether you want your parents to go with you to get the results. Most students (in fact, almost all) want their parents on hand. But it is up to you. You should do everything you can to minimise your stress levels.

In the days and weeks leading up to results day, think about planning some distractions for yourself. Use this time for community service projects, extracurricular activities, career training, gainful employment, or some combination of these.

'In the days and weeks leading up to results day, think about planning some distractions for yourself.'

Distraction will help pass the time

The day before results day, however, should be reserved for some quality time, rest and relaxation. Set this day aside regardless of what else you have been doing over the holidays.

A nice meal, a movie night, something like this is a good distraction for the night before. It sounds obvious, but get a good night's sleep before results day. Treat it as a kind of exam day. Exhaustion in any degree – even if it's just one bad night's sleep – is not going to help you with the emotional aspects of results day.

A good night's sleep and a sense of relaxation will also help promote a level head.

Going prepared on the day

You need to make sure that you have the right time, date and location information for your results day.

With a level head, you will be ready when it is time to go and pick up your AS and then A2 results and you will be able to process the information effectively.

Post the details on a calendar, set up reminders for you and your parents, just as with exams.

Just as with exam day appointments, you need to have back ups for getting to the appointed place at the appointed time. Even if you are planning on going with your parents to pick up your results, make sure that you have a back-up plan – another way for you to get there, someone else to go with you – if your parents are, for some reason, detained.

In addition to having a back-up plan, though, make sure you are also set up with the equipment you need to manage the information about your results.

Useful tools for results day include:

- A charged mobile phone with enough available minutes to call friends and family.
- A couple of pens and pencils.

- A reliable notepad.

- A calculator to check the totals for modules just in case there is an error.

If you are picking up A2 results, you should also pack your bag with the following:

- Results slips from AS.

- UCAS letter.

- Contact details for your university options.

- Copy of your personal statement and your reference if you have it.

- Contact details for your referee (and if you think it's likely you'll go into clearing, permission from your referee to pass on their details to universities).

- A copy of *The Telegraph*.

Having a back-up plan

Perhaps the smartest thing you can do for yourself on results day – both for AS and A2, is go in there with a clear plan to handle most if not all of the day's possible outcomes.

What do we mean by this?

Simple. Know your options. Write them down if necessary. In fact, it might be easier if you do write them down.

Use the following general template:

'If x happens I can do x, y, or z.'

For example:

'If I score poorly on one module, I can aim to make up points at A2, retake the module, or accept the grade and move on.'

Having a back-up plan will help you keep things in perspective. Remember, if you have completed your AS and A2 exams, nothing is set in stone about your A level grade. You don't have to close the book on your A levels unless you want to, unless you have the results you want.

'You don't have to close the book on your A levels unless you want to, unless you have the results you want.'

If you don't achieve the grades you want, instead of panicking, you will feel empowered by your options if you know in advance what they are.

Talk to your teachers about options for retaking modules or redoing coursework. Ask your school teacher about the possibility of repeating a year if that might be something that would help you. Ask questions before results day so you have the answers to work with.

Treat yourself, whatever the outcome

'Acknowledging the end of your A level experience, marked by your results day, will give you a sense of closure and help you prepare to move on to the next stage, whatever that happens to me.'

Whatever happens on results day, set aside time to celebrate what you have achieved over the two years of A levels. If you are reading this book at the beginning of your A level course, it might be difficult to gauge the importance of this step. But look back on your GCSE experience. Whatever your results, the work you put in was tremendous and deserves recognition.

Give yourself a break. Whether it is a meal out with family, a night out with friends, or a quiet evening to just relax.

Acknowledging the end of your A level experience, marked by your results day, will give you a sense of closure and help you prepare to move on to the next stage, whatever that happens to me.

Summing Up

- Results day is scary for just about everyone, but it is important to stay calm and give yourself a break.

- Make sure you get a good night's sleep and eat a healthy breakfast on results day morning.

- Make sure you double-check and write down the date, time and location for your results day.

- Have a back-up plan to get to your results day.

- Think about whether you want one or both of your parents to go with you (most students do).

- Have solutions for all foreseeable outcomes.

- Take a deep breath and reward yourself on results day, whatever the outcome.

Chapter Ten

What Now? Moving on From Your A Level Experience

After results day, there are decisions to be made. If you approach the situation early, though, you can go ahead and minimise a lot of the anxiety and uncertainty that tends to surround the question, 'What next?' for most A level students.

Applying to university

More than likely, you will be working on your UCAS application before you are finished with your A level examinations. In fact, you will probably be working on your UCAS application before you begin your A2 studies.

Although this isn't the place to go through the particulars of identifying an appropriate university placement, we can run through the basics of applying for university in the UK.

The main step in the UK university application is the UCAS form completion. Almost everything is done online these days, UCAS filing being no exception to that rule.

Registering with UCAS

To register with UCAS, go to the website at www.ucas.co.uk

You will need to register through your school or college.

You will need to have a code word or 'buzzword' from your school. This is a word that should only be used by applicants from your school and it will link your UCAS application directly to your school.

Make up a password for your UCAS application that you will remember and be sure to make a note of your UCAS-generated username. Usually it will be based on your initials and surname. It will also include a number. Write it down and don't forget it.

Once you have these details taken care of complete the rest of the UCAS form.

You will have to include your personal statement and pay the appropriate fees for your application.

You will need to fill in some personal data and you will also be asked to fill in your qualifications.

Listing your qualifications

You will be asked to enter the details of your qualifications. Remember to distinguish between GCSEs and Double Award GCSEs.

You will need to enter the grades you achieved, the month in which the exams were taken, and the year.

If you have already 'cashed' your AS levels, then you can also enter your GCE AS Level qualifications here, too.

'Cashing' means that you are not going to be taking a given subject at A2, and that you have essentially decided to use the results that you have without doing any additional work or review of them.

You will need to enter the subjects you are taking at GCE A levels and for all qualifications that have not yet been cashed in, you will have a grade 'Pending'.

'Make up a password for your UCAS application that you will remember and be sure to make a note of your UCAS generated username.'

Application deadlines to be aware of

It can be difficult to stay on top of the various important dates for UCAS but there are a couple of deadlines you should be aware of as you are working through AS and A2:

- From June onwards in Year 12, you will be able to register online for UCAS.

- The deadline for Oxford and Cambridge applications, as well as for medicine, dentistry and veterinary science/medicine applicants is 15th October.

- The deadline for all other applicants is 15th January. Applications should have reached UCAS by this date. If UCAS does not have your application by this date, you can still apply for university but you will not receive the same consideration as those who submitted their application by 15th January.

- 31st March is the date that most universities send out their offers/declinations to candidates.

- The final deadline for universities to give you a decision, if you applied before 15th January, is 8th May.

- You must have your applications in by 30th June to receive immediate consideration. If you submit your application after this, your application will be held for clearing.

- Clearing starts in August.

Dealing with your results

The first 'what next?' after results day concerns your actual A level results.

Once you have your results in hand and know what they are, you will be dealing with one of several scenarios.

Making your offer

If you have made your offer – i.e. scored enough points overall and achieved the grades you need, you can celebrate!

If your first choice university has asked you to call in and confirm anything, go ahead and do so at this point. Since most universities do not ask you to confirm when you have made your offer, though, don't call unless you have been told to.

Instead, call anyone and everyone else to share the good news and start looking forward to the next phase of your life.

Missing your firm offer

If you haven't achieved the grades to earn your first offer, first of all, don't panic and try not to be too disappointed at this stage.

There is a chance that your first choice may actually still accept you even if you did not get the grades they asked for.

The first thing you are going to want to do to follow up when you have missed your firm offer is visit the UCAS website service that is set up to track your results (UCAS Track).

This system may take some time to update but it will be a checkpoint to see what your status is after your results have come in.

Track may tell you one of two things:

'If you have lost your offer because of your grades, keep in mind that you may be able to make a case to your university of choice and earn that place back.'

- That your offer is deemed 'unconditional', in which case, missing your target grades is no major problem for you.

- That you have not gotten your place after all.

If you have lost your offer because of your grades, keep in mind that you may be able to make a case to your university of choice and earn that place back. For instance, if you have new information to provide which the university is not already aware of, including any mitigating circumstances about your exams and results, or if you have just missed your grades by a few points, you may be able to hold your place after all.

Mitigating circumstances will usually require your school to make contact with the university directly and as soon as possible.

Because universities don't actually receive a breakdown of your grades, i.e. the UMS marks, it may be worth communicating with them if you were only a few points from hitting your target grades. It may be worth seeing if they will reconsider.

Of course, you probably have at least one 'insurance' or back-up offer to work with. If you have made this offer and are happy with it, you can still close the book on your A level experience and get ready to move on to the next thing.

Going through clearing

If you missed your firm and insurance offers by quite a bit, you are going to want to go through what is known as 'clearing'. The 'clearing' system helps university students find alternative vacancies if they have not managed to secure a place at their chosen university. If neither of your offers (firm or insurance) would accept you with lower grades, clearing is the best option for you.

But don't panic.

There's lots of choice in clearing.

If you can't find the right fit in terms of course and university, don't panic about that either. You can always take a gap year or think about retaking a couple of A level units.

Talk to your parents and your teachers about this situation. Give yourself some time if you think you need it to remain calm and level-headed.

'Going straight to university after your A levels may be the best option for you but there is no harm in thinking things through and making a decision that is truly informed.'

Considering your options

So far, we have only mentioned university as an option after A levels. While it is the most common option for A level students, it is by no means the only option.

Once you have your results in hand, consider the pros and cons of, for instance, taking a gap year.

Going straight to university after your A levels may be the best option for you and you may be set up to do it, but there is no harm in thinking things through and making a decision that is truly informed.

Summing Up

▪ Celebrate what you have achieved with A levels and then be ready for the next step.

▪ The next step for most people is university but take a minute to consider your options.

▪ Consider the pros and cons of a gap year.

▪ Consider your university choices now that you have your results in hand.

▪ Even if things have not turned out as you have expected, know that you have options.

Glossary

A levels

The term commonly used to refer to the Advanced Level General Certificate of Education. These are standardised tests used in most parts of the UK and other places around the world to assess and grade students prior to university entry. 'A levels' are comprised of AS and A2 exams (see below).

AS levels

The term commonly used to refer to the Advanced (AS) Subsidiary GCE Level.

A2

The term, A2, refers to the second lot of modules and the second year of study for the A level. When you complete A2s for a given subject, you are completing an Advanced Level General Certificate of Education in that subject.

AS12 Letter

This is a confirmation letter that is sent out by UCAS. It tells you that your place at a university has been confirmed. It will also detail your course choice and is the final confirmation that you have your university placement.

Clearing

Service provided by UCAS that applicants can access to find alternative vacancies if they have ben unsuccessful in securing a place at their chosen university

Module

This is a unit of study that is assessed by written examination and provided with a numerical score at A level. Currently, most A level courses (AS and A2) comprise of two modules each or four for a total A level qualification. Some subjects (sciences) have six modules instead of four.

Revision

Revision or 'revising' is the process of revisiting or reviewing information that you have learned in the past to test your knowledge and prepare for examinations.

Specifications

This is the term used to refer to the syllabus or requirements outlined for the achievement of an AS or A level. Each of the five exam boards that test for A levels and AS qualifications offer specific specifications for each of their AS or A level subjects.

UCAS

The Universities and Colleges Admissions Service (UCAS) is the British admission service for students applying to university and college

Help List

A level Resources for Students

National Academic Recognition IC, Ecctis 2000

Oriel House, Oriel Road, Cheltenham, GL50 1XP
Tel: 0871 330 7033
www.naric.org.uk
This is the national agency based in the UK that is officially responsible for providing information, advice and expert opinion on vocational, academic and professional skills and qualifications from over 180 countries worldwide.

OCR Coventry Office

Progress House, Westwood Way, Coventry, CV4 8JQ
Tel: 02476 851509
Email: vocational.qualifications@ocr.org.uk

OCR Cymru

Windsor House, Windsor Lane, Caerdydd/Cardiff, Wales, CF10 3DE
Tel: 02920 537 810
Email: ocr-cymru@ocr.org.uk
www.ocr.org.uk/cymru
This office provides a range of specialist support services to customers across Wales. These services include advice, quality assurance support and training.

OCR Head Office – Cambridge

1 Hills Road, Cambridge CB1 2EU
Tel: 01223 553998
Email: general.qualifications@ocr.org.uk
www.ocr.org.uk

OCR Ireland

Riverwood House, Newforge Lane, Belfast, Northern Ireland BT9 5NW
Tel: 02890 669 797
Email: ocr-ireland@ocr.org.uk
www.ocr.org.uk/ireland/
This office provides a range of specialist support services to customers in both Northern Ireland and the Republic of Ireland. These services include advice, quality assurance support and training.

UCAS

Customer Service Unit, UCAS, PO Box 28, Cheltenham GL52 3LZ
Tel: 0871 468 0 468
Email: enquiries@ucas.ac.uk
www.ucas.co.uk
This is the organisation responsible for managing applications to higher education courses in the UK.

University of Cambridge International Examinations

Tel: 01223 553554
Email: international@cie.org.uk
www.cie.org.uk
This is the Cambridge University exam board contact for the United Kingdom, Ireland and the Faroe Islands.